T0334698

Cambridge Elements ≡

Elements in Publishing and Book Culture
edited by
Samantha J. Rayner
University College London
Leah Tether
University of Bristol

MUDIE'S SELECT LIBRARY AND THE SHELF LIFE OF THE NINETEENTH-CENTURY NOVEL

Karen Wade
University College Dublin

CAMBRIDGE
UNIVERSITY PRESS

Shaftesbury Road, Cambridge CB2 8EA, United Kingdom

One Liberty Plaza, 20th Floor, New York, NY 10006, USA

477 Williamstown Road, Port Melbourne, VIC 3207, Australia

314–321, 3rd Floor, Plot 3, Splendor Forum, Jasola District Centre,
New Delhi – 110025, India

103 Penang Road, #05–06/07, Visioncrest Commercial, Singapore 238467

Cambridge University Press is part of Cambridge University Press & Assessment,
a department of the University of Cambridge.

We share the University's mission to contribute to society through the pursuit of
education, learning and research at the highest international levels of excellence.

www.cambridge.org
Information on this title: www.cambridge.org/9781009479004

DOI: 10.1017/9781009478991

First published 2025

A catalogue record for this publication is available from the British Library

ISBN 978-1-009-47900-4 Paperback
ISSN 2514-8524 (online)
ISSN 2514-8516 (print)

Mudie's Select Library and the Shelf Life of the Nineteenth-Century Novel

Elements in Publishing and Book Culture

DOI: 10.1017/9781009478991
First published online: January 2025

Karen Wade
University College Dublin

Author for correspondence: Karen Wade, karen.wade@ucd.ie

ABSTRACT: Mudie's Select Library was a major nineteenth-century literary institution. Substantially larger than its competitors, the library leveraged regional and global distribution networks and close commercial ties with publishers which allowed it to maintain a key position within the British publishing industry. In its heyday, it was widely believed that novelists and publishers were required to conform to aesthetic, moral, and formal standards established by Mudie's, or risk the rejection and consequent failure of their books. However, the lack of a comprehensive study of the library's holdings leaves open questions about what the library actually stocked, and to what extent the library could determine a novel's fate. This Element describes a data analysis of a collection of Mudie's catalogues spanning eighty years, in order to reassess understandings of the library's role in the nineteenth-century publishing industry. This title is also available as Open Access on Cambridge Core.

This Element also has a video abstract: www.cambridge.org/mudiesselectlibrary

KEYWORDS: Mudie's, nineteenth-century novels, nineteenth-century libraries, nineteenth-century British publishing, library catalogues

ISBNs: 9781009479004 (PB), 9781009478991 (OC)
ISSNs: 2514-8524 (online), 2514-8516 (print)

Contents

1 Introduction   1

2 Accession, Retention, and Delisting of Novels   22

3 Selection in Practice: A Ten-Year Sample of
   Published Novels and Their Shelf Lives   44

4 Cents and Censorship: Representation in Mudie's
   and Its Impacts   56

5 Conclusion   83

   References   86

1 Introduction

'...Mudie supplies us with all our worldly and spiritual knowledge, barring what we pick up from our morning paper. We read everything – theological works, theosophic works, translations of the ancients, like Homer and Cicero, essays on Socialism, histories of heathen religions and society novels.' 'By Jove! what a pot-pourri; and which is most to your taste?' 'That depends much upon my frame of mind and the weather, but I fear my taste is so far demoralised as to experience the greatest amount of enjoyment in a really good novel.'

Miss Blanchard of Chicago (1892), Albert Kevill-Davies

1.1 'No Library So Good': The Origins, Development, and Influence of Mudie's Select Library

In 1842, Charles Edward Mudie, the proprietor of a modest stationery shop in Holborn, London, began loaning out a small collection of his own favourite books to discerning customers. A second-generation stationer, Mudie was described by his patrons as studious, thoughtful, and 'of somewhat "advanced" theological views', and his shop attracted a small but dedicated cohort of readers who, as one of their members later recalled, 'gladly availed themselves of what was then a unique collection' (Espinasse 1893: 27). While circulating libraries of the late eighteenth and early nineteenth centuries were commonly viewed as suppliers of heavily thumbed novels of debatable literary and moral value, Mudie offered modern books and periodicals 'of a progressive kind', including works by American transcendental writers such as Margaret Fuller and Ralph Waldo Emerson (Griest 1970: 17). The success of this venture led Mudie to expand the library side of his business, moving to larger quarters at the corner of New Oxford and Museum Streets in 1851. In 1860, the library acquired neighbouring sites in order to provide storage for what was now a vast assemblage of books and to house its by now greatly expanded administrative apparatus: boardrooms and staff offices, a bustling Export Department, rebinding and retail facilities, and the public lending counters of the library's iconic 'Great Hall'. In 1894, *Good Words* described this as 'a spacious and very lofty apartment lighted from a domed roof' and lined with galleries of books, and it served the needs of a 'constant stream of readers or their representatives [passing] in and out of the place' (Preston 1894: 669). Located within visual distance of another key Victorian cultural institution, the British Museum – with its own iconic Reading Room – Mudie's was now at the heart of the literary life of the British Empire.[1]

Over the course of the ninety years in which it was active, the institution now known as Mudie's Select Library became Britain's preeminent circulating library. The cornerstone of its success was the combination of relatively affordable subscription rates – a basic subscription could be had for just one guinea a year, which undercut rivals by a substantial margin[2] – and an expansive, if not exhaustive, collection of titles that few competitors could attempt to rival, and which was constantly promoted to the public via newspaper advertisements and circulars. By design, Mudie's did not stock *every* book that might be requested by subscribers, with specific accession policies (as well as physical space restrictions) determining which works the library accessioned, listed, and circulated. Still, a sufficient number of Victorian readers found its selection satisfactory for it to be generally considered the most subscribed-to circulating library of nineteenth-century Britain.[3] At its peak, Mudie's was estimated to have 50,000 subscribers, and the library circulated books

---

[1] *London Society* called attention to this juxtaposition in November 1869: 'A great value belongs to "Mudie's" as the necessary complement and supplement to our hugest reading-room in the world. For at the British Museum a man can get almost any book he can possibly desire, with the exception, which is often like the roc's egg in Aladdin's palace, he cannot obtain an entirely new book. But here Mr. Mudie, like an amicably-disposed magician, comes to the rescue' (*London Society* 1869: 448).

[2] Jacobs (2006) notes that the annual membership fee for circulating libraries in the years 1730–1842 generally stood at around double the purchase price of a normal three-volume novel; Mudie's lowest-tier subscription of a guinea represented around two thirds of the price of a novel.

[3] Writing in 1893, Espinasse supposed it to be 'the largest circulating library in the world' (27).

(both new and second-hand) through global distribution channels which were based upon pre-existing trade and transport networks of the British Empire. Smaller libraries in India, South Africa, Australia, and New Zealand were stocked with books bought from Mudie's (Preston 1894: 627), and the library even offered packages of novels aimed at ship's captains, for their passengers' amusement (Mudie's Select Library 1862: 27).

As Vie Carlisle asserts in the quote from *Miss Blanchard of Chicago* cited earlier, a subscription to Mudie's could satisfy readers of a wide variety of tastes. In 1864, a columnist for the *Illustrated Times* noted that despite occasionally failing to acquire a specific title from Mudie's due to the library's capricious acquisition policies, 'I remain a subscriber because I can find no library so good, or nearly so good' (Lounger at the Clubs 1864: 7). Serving readers from branch libraries in Manchester and Birmingham as well as from its main site in central London, the library also delivered books to readers outside of metropolitan areas via its popular parcel delivery system. By the 1890s, the library was sending out around 1,000 boxes by rail or other carriers every week (Preston 1894: 675), and many nineteenth-century commentators fondly recall the arrival of the weekly or monthly 'Mudie box'.[4] Remaining faithful to its roots as a theological and philosophical library, Mudie's stocked a compelling selection of non-fiction titles in genres such as history, biography, travel, religion, and science, as well as periodicals, and was regarded as a valuable resource by scholars and researchers, in addition to those who read primarily for leisure. However, fiction, then as now, represented a key attraction for library subscribers. A significant portion – generally around 30 per cent to 40 per cent – of all titles listed in the

---

[4] In just one of many examples, Florence Brandreth, the narrator of *A Troubled Stream*, describes her happy-ever-after as follows: 'An unfettered country life, with occasional visits to Town, or some cheerful sea-side place; a bright and happy home; horses, carriages, and sufficient money for all my wants and wishes; my poor people and school-children to attend to; my piano, my drawing-box, and books from Mudie's; and above all, my dear, kind husband, and my darling children; what more can I desire?' (Hardcastle 1866: III, 270).

catalogues consisted of novels, while Charles Edward Mudie's own estimate was that fiction comprised around 42 per cent of the physical volumes held by the library (Mudie 1860).[5]

Although they did not represent the lion's share of the collection, and were often less prominently advertised, novels were believed to be a key driver of library subscriptions, due in part to a notorious and much-discussed quirk of the British publishing industry: the preference of libraries and publishers for issuing the first edition of a new novel in three volumes. While it was considered the most prestigious format, the 'triple-decker' was costly to produce, and from the 1820s to the 1890s it was typically offered to the public at one and a half guineas, or 31s 6d.[6] Because such a price was well outside the budget of most readers, few copies of a three-volume first edition were sold directly to the public. Instead, the initial print run of most books would be bought primarily by circulating libraries such as Mudie's, W. H. Smith's, and their competitors, who could expect discount rates from publishers in exchange for bulk orders, and who then effectively controlled access to the books until a cheaper second edition was issued.[7]

---

[5] Because this study has not included a full survey of Mudie's non-fiction listings, it is not possible to state precisely how much of the library's collection was fiction and how much was non-fiction. However, our estimates based on the number of catalogue pages devoted to each category indicate that fiction titles made up around 31 per cent of Mudie's stock in 1848, rising to 42 per cent in 1885. In a letter to *The Athenaeum*, 6 October 1860, C. E. Mudie (1860) reported that 165,445 of the 391,083 volumes purchased since 1858 were fiction. Works of history and biography made up 22.3 per cent, travel and adventure 12.9 per cent, and miscellaneous works ('including science, religion and the latest Reviews') represented 22.5 per cent of recent acquisitions.

[6] Production costs played a role in this high price, but it was also a matter of convention which was maintained for almost seventy years despite significant changes in book production. The first book to command such a price was Walter Scott's *Kenilworth* in 1821, and three-volume novels were still being listed at a guinea and a half into the 1890s; *Miss Blanchard of Chicago* (1892) is one such example.

[7] Data compiled by David Finkelstein from the archives of publishers Blackwood & Sons, Smith, Elder & Co., John Murray, and Bentley, representing purchases in

As a consequence, the maintenance of the triple-decker has been widely regarded as a form of price fixing between the libraries and the publishers; as Roberts (2006) comments, 'the 31s 6d price was never the basis of exchange – indeed, the high price functioned solely as a deterrent to individual buyers' (3). Non-fiction was not tied to such specific price conventions, yet it could be equally inaccessible to the average buyer due to cost. For example, the third and fourth volumes of Macaulay's *History of England* retailed at 36 shillings for the pair upon their joint publication in 1855; Mudie's placed an order for 2,500 copies of this work.[8] As Gladstone commented in an 1852 debate on the topic of repealing the duty on paper, '[t]he purchase of new publications is scarcely ever attempted by anybody. You go into the houses of your friends, and unless they buy books of which they are in professional want, or happen to be persons of extraordinary wealth, you don't find copies of new publications on their tables purchased by themselves, but you find something from the circulating library' (Gladstone 1852: n.p.).[9] Similarly, a columnist known as the Lounger at

the years around 1860, indicates that Mudie's frequently 'subscribed' (placed orders for) a healthy percentage of the available copies of novels published by these firms. Sales to Mudie's accounted for at least 20 per cent of a novel's print run in three-quarters of cases. Occasionally, as in the case of Nathaniel Hawthorne's *Transformation* and Robert Dwarris Gibney's *My Escape from the Mutinies of Oudh*, the library might take half or more of the available copies (Finkelstein 1993: 41, 45).

[8] Griest (1970) describes popular prejudice against single-volume books, arguing that they tended to be seen as 'cheap reprints' or 'railway novels', and that such beliefs 'reinforced the distinction of the original', adding to the prestige of multivolume works (48). The enormous success of cheap reprints and railway novels suggests that this prejudice may not have had the determining effect that Griest describes. It may, however, have influenced the desire of publishers to produce both fiction and non-fiction in multivolume or 'dignity' editions, at least in their initial print runs.

[9] Gladstone's Paper Duty Repeal Bill, which was defeated by the House of Lords in 1860, was finally forced through the following year, resulting in reduced prices for newspapers and other publications and resulting in a 'greatly expanded mass audience' (Altick 1957: 356–7).

the Clubs grumbled in the *Illustrated Times* that 'on two occasions I have had to *buy* the book' – but only when the selection at Mudie's failed him (Lounger at the Clubs 1864: 7).

As a consequence of these factors, Mudie's and its direct competitors were believed to play a key gatekeeping role in Victorian publishing, both by those working in the industry at the time and by later scholars and commentators, and a natural corollary of that belief was that the library's powers of 'selection' had widespread implications for literature more generally. A view which was widely held – and, indeed, emphasised by Charles Edward Mudie and his staff as a selling point – was that the library would only supply works which conformed to the library's standards of respectability, and that books which dealt with potentially fraught topics, such as issues of sexual morality or religious controversy, risked exclusion. Length and format, too, were widely believed to be generally dictated by the libraries. Until recently, conventional wisdom held that the major circulating libraries colluded with British publishers to publish and circulate as many novels as possible in the expensive 'triple-decker' format, in order to maintain a monopoly over new fiction that was beneficial to the interests of both parties.[10] With this system in place, avid readers could not avoid the necessity of a subscription to a major library, nor could writers or publishers circumvent the libraries and their preferences. Gladstone and the Lounger at the Clubs were not the only critics of this state of affairs. Writers such as George Moore, Charles Reade, and James McGrigor Allan publicly complained that Mudie's suppressed free trade, free speech, and literary innovation, and debates regarding the library's gatekeeping broke out on a number of occasions in the popular press.[11] Some modern critics have argued that the preferences

[10] See Griest (1970), for example – 'the library actually preferred nominally high prices as a kind of insurance that readers would be compelled to borrow' (11).

[11] See Moore's (1976) *Literature at Nurse* and Charles Reade's (1883) *Readiana*. James McGrigor Allan printed an open letter to Mudie which is preserved in his Royal Literary Fund application and is also cited in some contemporary newspapers (McGrigor Allan 1864). For a detailed survey of newspaper debates on Mudie's, see Katz (2017).

of the library had a homogenising effect upon Victorian fiction, tending to encourage inflated word counts, conventional moralising, and general blandness, and perhaps serving to entirely suppress worthy works of fiction.[12] Yet others argued that there were benefits, too, claiming that those on the creative end were guaranteed some kind of market for their publications by the libraries, while readers were assured of a steady supply of new books. As *London Society* reported in an 1869 piece titled 'Going to Mudie's', 'The literary appetite has, in part, been created by the literary supply, which lends it both satisfaction and incitement' (*London Society* 1869: 448). Even the library's reputed censorship was, at times, defended. Some contemporary writers preferred the three-volume format and agreed that there was a need for literary fiction to adhere to some form of moral standard;[13] more recently, bibliographical scholar Sara Keith has argued that the library system, with its sophisticated apparatuses for marketing and disseminating fiction, was at least partly responsible for the success of many of the works of classic literature that are considered part of the Victorian canon (Keith 1973).

In recent years, some key aspects of this understanding of Mudie's, and of the centrality of its place in literary history, have been reconsidered by modern scholarship. As Section 1.2 describes, studies have indicated that the triple-decker novel was neither as ubiquitous nor as unerringly profitable a format as has generally been assumed. Mudie's much-discussed reputation for 'selection' has also been challenged by research which indicates that commercial considerations – including the

---

[12] Coustillas argues that the system encouraged 'the average novelist of no particular merit' to write longer works that would command a higher price from publishers, but that 'as three-volume fiction found a notable portion of its readers among the idle females of the middle-classes whose view of life was narrow, the artist's freedom in the choice and treatment of his subject thus was severely restricted' (Moore 1976: 11, 13).

[13] Griest (1970) describes a range of views on the subject of morality and censorship (137–40); she also notes a passionate defence of the three-volume format by M. E. Braddon, who had published forty-seven such works over the course of thirty-three years (206).

library's own current financial status – was often more influential upon its decision to take or exclude a book than aesthetic or moral standards. Such reassessments, many of which are based on the analysis of bibliographic and archival source materials, represent a significant expansion in our understanding of the library. This Element describes a project which has compiled a contemporary source of information on the library – eight of its catalogues, spanning a sixty-year period – in order to contribute to this conversation. This work has been conducted in the spirit of what literary historian Katherine Bode has described as 'data-rich literary history', in which historical data is used to assist in investigating 'the cultural and material contexts in which literature was produced', seeking to 'challenge and move beyond the literary canons that organize perceptions of past literature in the present' (Bode 2018: 3). In keeping with Bode's assertion that the articulation of the complex relationships between 'documentary record, digitization, data curation, and historical analysis' is imperative, this work attempts to 'read' the catalogues not in isolation but in conversation with other sources of archival information and data, and as complex, often ambiguous documents which served a variety of purposes other than simply providing information to a reading public.

In 2009, Simon Eliot suggested that with 'world enough and time', the catalogues might be able to answer question such as 'what range of texts was readily available to the middle-class borrower, and how extensive was the title collection for one specific author compared to another?' (Eliot 2009: 33). In digitising and collating the complete fiction listings of eight catalogues published between 1848 and 1907, it has indeed been possible to enumerate the specific range of texts which were available to the library's subscribers – or, at least, which were openly advertised via the catalogues – and to compare the shelf space which was afforded to different authors. These listings, which are now available both as a dataset and as a searchable reference resource titled Mudie's Library Online, also prompt questions about the role of the library in its heyday, as well as its impact upon the careers and lives of individuals working within the publishing and circulating library systems.

1.2 Scholarship

As Guinevere Griest asserts throughout her landmark history of Mudie's Select Library *Mudie's Circulating Library and the Victorian Novel*, it is impossible to fully understand the development of the nineteenth-century British novel without a thorough understanding of the systems within which it originated and was circulated to the reading public. More than fifty years on, Griest's monograph remains the foundational work of scholarship on Mudie's; it is also the most thorough, drawing on a wealth of contemporary sources in order to delineate the social and economic contexts within which Mudie's functioned. Her work argues that the major circulating libraries represented an insurmountable, determining force within the British publishing industry: partly due to their ability to 'embody a part of the Victorian temperament' and partly because of their purchasing power, 'all efforts to overthrow their supremacy or to change the form and price of the novel were ineffectual' (Griest 1970: 4). While Griest is primarily focused upon the role and experience of novels within the library, she argues that every facet of nineteenth-century British literature was impacted by the preferences and workflows of Mudie's and the other major circulating libraries, from the word counts that novelists were required to adhere to (at least 900 pages for most triple-deckers, although publishers could pad these by adding extra-wide margins) to the distribution networks that took British books to and beyond the borders of the British Empire.

Key to Griest's history is a detailed account of the three-volume novel, and the ways in which its fortunes intersected with those of the major circulating libraries. Her primary argument, which has influenced much subsequent scholarship, is that the major circulating libraries strongly preferred novels to be published in three volumes, with the understanding that this lent them an economic advantage by allowing a single book to be borrowed by three readers at the same time. Griest's work also gives extensive consideration to the concept of 'selection', or the library's assertion of its right to purchase and circulate only those works which were considered by its management to adhere to prevailing aesthetic and moral standards. Sometimes described as the 'young woman' standard (suggesting that all novels must be suitable for what was deemed by Victorians to be the most vulnerable, impressionable reader), these strictures were poorly defined and subject to change over time, and were decried by many working writers (such as Francis Power Cobbe) who found their works 'tabooed' by Mudie's or who were required to pad their novels with extra material to make up an additional volume (as occurred with Elizabeth Gaskell's *Mary Barton*).[14] Despite such criticism, Griest argues, the libraries were often beneficial to writers and publishers in that they provided a 'guaranteed market' for novels: since the British public was so acclimatised to borrowing rather than buying their novels, 'authors who accepted the standards were virtually guaranteed at least a minimum audience', while those who attempted to circumvent the library system were 'severely handicapped' (Griest 1970: 147).

Subsequent scholarship, at times less nuanced than Griest's, has generally endorsed her depiction of the library's gatekeeping as being based upon a 'young woman' standard and maintained via access to a 'guaranteed market'. In his introduction to a modern edition of a critique of Mudie's, George Moore's *Literature at Nurse*, Pierre Coustillas argues that the library's 'selection' policies were directly detrimental to the progress of literature, stating that 'as three-volume fiction found a notable portion of its readers among the idle females of the middle-classes whose view of life was narrow, the artist's freedom in the choice and treatment of his subject thus was severely restricted' (Moore 1976: 13). Conversely, in 1973 Sara Keith (1973) argued that 'if Mudie's can serve as an index of popularity, one might generalize from its history that selectivity is a good thing as long as the selection is intelligently made' (372). Keith's and Coustillas's accounts of 'selection', while almost diametrically opposed, both partake of the understanding that Mudie's' preferences were highly influential upon the fiction of the later nineteenth century, and this can also be found in other accounts of publishing phenomena.[15]

---

[14] In 1894 Cobbe recalled young women readers of the 1860s being dissuaded from borrowing her works by Mudie's staff members, apparently due to their impropriety. Gaskell was asked to expand her debut novel to allow it to be published in two volumes; while the request was made by Chapman and Hall, Griest views it as part of a the general pressure placed on novelists to publish in a multivolume format for the sake of the libraries (Griest 1970: 215, 99).

[15] See, for example, Fryckstedt (1995: 24); Shattock (2012: 7); Sutherland (1976: 25–30).

In representing contemporary perceptions of Mudie's, Griest's work is invaluable. However, evidence from the library catalogue data suggests a need to reassess some of her contentions, as other scholarship has already indicated. From the 1990s onward, studies examining various sources of data on the library have posed challenges to aspects of her account. Given its controversial nature, 'selection' has understandably undergone particular scrutiny. David Finkelstein's examination of the records of a number of major nineteenth-century publishers revealed that Mudie's weathered a financial crisis after a period of intense expansion in the early 1860s (Finkelstein 1993). On the brink of collapse, the library was secretly bailed out by a number of publishing houses; for a time, its business affairs, including the nature and quantity of its book orders, were strongly influenced by these firms. Similarly, Colclough's 2016 examination of *Mudie's Library Circular* and other advertising materials indicated that book selection and circulation could be influenced by factors other than the library's declared standards. Despite reviewers' concerns about the suitability of sensation novels for general audiences, their enormous popularity with readers meant that they were strategically promoted by the library in times of financial stress, in order to encourage subscriptions. Assumptions about the three-volume novel, particularly concerning its prominence and profitability, have also come into question. Eliot's 2009 examination of a selection of Mudie's catalogues notes that at no point were three-volume novels the most common in Mudie's fiction collection. Single-volume novels were consistently present in higher numbers than multivolume works; even in 1889, the year that Eliot identifies as its peak, the triple-decker only represents 40 per cent of the collection, while single volumes comprise 47 per cent (Eliot 2009: 36). Nesta's 2007 consideration of the economics of the three-volume novel, meanwhile, argues that three-volume novels often made a loss for publishers and did not encourage new writers into the market, and that British readers were avid purchasers of books in various formats as long as they were reasonably priced (Nesta 2007: 65–6). In contrast, Bassett's large-scale 2020 survey of nineteenth-century fiction publishing argued that Bentley's, at least, found triple-deckers to be consistently profitable but also suggests that while multivolume fiction was popular throughout the nineteenth century, it rarely comprised a majority of titles and its market share was in decline from at least the 1880s (Bassett 2020).

Such findings suggest that other popular understandings of Mudie's economic, literary, and social impact may reward re-examination, particularly when new tools and datasets become available. Given the loss of the library's business records upon its closure in 1937, a source of data such as the combined catalogue provides another avenue for considering the experience of books and their authors in the library. Were contemporary fears about censorship merited? Did the library's role as gatekeeper impact upon the availability and consequent success of books, or did it simply mirror the moral tastes and preferences of the public? What factors affected the provision of fictional works to the nineteenth-century public, and how do these impact upon current understandings of Victorian novels – and the Victorian period?

1.3 Methodology and Data
1.3.1 The Combined Catalogues

The catalogues on which this work is based are available as an open access dataset (see Wade et al. 2024). This Element is based on version 1.0. The dataset is comprised of the complete fiction listings of eight catalogues, which were published by Mudie's between 1848 and 1907 (see Table 1). While the information they contain tends to vary from catalogue to catalogue, they consistently provide the titles and (usually) the names of the author or authors of each work; this information forms the backbone of the dataset. The earliest catalogue, 1848–9, is a simple list of titles and authors, but from the 1850s onward, catalogues also provide information about format (namely, the number of volumes) and book size (generally quarto, octavo, and duodecimo).[16] Where available, some additional information has been added to the dataset by the project team, including information in relation to author identity (such as gender, pseudonym status, multiple authorship, etc.) The dataset records whether a work was listed by title, author, or both, allowing for an accurate count of the number

---

[16] The 1907 catalogue does not provide information on size or volumes. This may be due to the sheer number of listings provided in this year (the catalogue is printed in two columns, to save space), but it may also be related to the transition toward single-volume editions as standard, which had begun in 1894.

Table 1 Catalogues in the study, with number of unique fiction titles.

Catalogue year	Number of unique titles
1848–9	797
1857	1,257
1860	1,428
1865	2,198
1876	3,526
1885	4,858
1895	8,393
1907	15,418
Combined	22,040

of works in a catalogue, as well as identifying titles which were deemed important enough to be listed twice. The final catalogue in the collection, which dates to 1907, also provides a thematic index which provides categorisations for around a third of the library's fiction holdings in that year. Throughout this Element, I have referred to the complete dataset as 'the combined catalogues'.

The dataset was initially created by extracting the text from scanned copies of Mudie's library catalogues using optical character recognition, consolidating these onto a single spreadsheet, and then conducting an extensive manual inspection for errors and duplications. Some catalogues (1857, 1860, 1865, 1876, and 1907) had been digitised and made available by their holding institutions and were available online as scanned PDFs; for the years 1885 and 1895, members of the project team purchased and scanned original copies of the catalogues.[17] Finally, with the permission of the Guildhall Library and the London Metropolitan Archives, a copy of the rare 1848–9 catalogue was photographed, and its listings were then added to the dataset manually.

[17] For more information, see 'Data User Guide, Mudie's Select Library 1848–1907, v1.0' in Wade et al. (2024).

This sample of eight Mudie's catalogues represents an attempt to create a roughly even chronological spread of listings, while working within the constraints of what is available. The earliest known (and perhaps the first) Mudie's catalogue is the 1848–9 edition, of which just two examples are known to survive; for the first thirty years of the library's history, catalogues were printed irregularly and may not have all survived. Meanwhile, from the 1880s to around 1900, Mudie's printed catalogues on an almost yearly basis, and many examples of these are extant in archives around the world.

Compiled as part of a larger project, VICTEUR (European Migrants in the Victorian Imagination), the Mudie's dataset was originally created as an aid to working with a large-scale, unstructured collection of around 40,000 digitised volumes dating to the nineteenth century. This massive collection, the British Library Nineteenth-Century Corpus (BL19), while representing a valuable resource for digital literary scholars, has accurately been described as 'if not random [then] at least arbitrary in its contents' (Ahnert et al. 2023: 32; also see Leavy et al. 2019 for the VICTEUR project's use of BL19).[18] In the spirit of Sara Keith's description of Mudie's Select Library as 'an index of popularity', the VICTEUR team decided to use Mudie's catalogues to help identify fictional works within the BL19 collection that were widely available to the reading public in the nineteenth century. During the course of this work, it became apparent that Mudie's' catalogues contained a wealth of information that would be of

---

[18] This collection, sometimes known as Microsoft Books, was the result of a short-lived collaboration between the British Library Labs and Microsoft, which resulted in the digitisation of a substantial but non-representative sample of books from the British Library. While the collection's approximately 40,000 digitised volumes include substantial numbers of works of fiction, travel, history, drama, and poetry, other prominent nineteenth-century genres such as religious works appear underrepresented, and it is difficult to determine whether these books were read by or even accessible to a wide audience. As Ahnert et al. (2023) note, 'this heterogeneity means that users need to think carefully about whether it meets the needs of their research' (32).

broader interest, and for this reason an online platform has been created to allow users to consult the catalogues.[19]

The catalogues provide a source of data on the library's history and functioning which is invaluable given the dearth of surviving archival materials, and a number of scholars have previously undertaken bibliographic work which incorporates catalogue data from Mudie's, sometimes focusing on a specific area. Simon Eliot's 2009 article, which describes listings from a sample of twelve catalogues, is the most extensive previously published survey, while other examinations of single or multiple catalogues have been undertaken by Clarence Gohdes (1942; on American literature), Sara Keith (1955), Monica Fryckstedt (1987; 1995), and Marie-Françoise Cachin (2012; on French literature).[20] However, the library's fiction listings have not previously been collated on a large scale. Eliot's comment that 'with world enough and time' a complete survey of Mudie's catalogues might yield insights is relevant here (Eliot 2009: 33): even with the aid of twenty-first-century technology, compiling an accurate, consolidated Mudie's catalogue spanning multiple different editions was a very labour-intensive project.

At the time of writing, the Mudie's dataset comprises listing information on 22,040 unique titles, many of which appear in two or more of the eight catalogues in the sample, and 6,006 authors. The original catalogues show occasional variation in titles (which may be truncated or, more rarely, include a subtitle) and author names (such as pseudonym use or name changes). The library's custom of listing certain works twice, by title and also by author, provided a further complication. While exhaustive efforts have been made to provide an accurate representation of the library data, errors certainly remain: revised versions of the data will be added to the published dataset as they become available. Currently, however, the dataset

---

[19] Mudie's Library Online can be consulted at http://erdos.ucd.ie/mudies/. The dataset itself is available for download via Harvard Dataverse (see Wade et al. 2024)

[20] The Sara Keith archive at the library of the University of London lists an unpublished 'title index to principal works of fiction in circulation and their occurrence in the Mudie catalogues for 1876 and 1884' (1955).

provides the most complete and extensive digital record of the fiction holdings of this library during the nineteenth century.

In the creation of a digital record of what these catalogues contain, it became apparent that their changing size, shape, and weight also bears physical witness to changes in the library over time. The 1848 catalogue is a mere pamphlet, listing a few thousand titles in total; new acquisitions from 1849 were added with the aid of an appendix which was stapled in at the back. As Table 1 indicates, the library's fiction collection doubled roughly every decade, and by 1907 the catalogue was a large, heavy, double-columned book, featuring a complex multi-part system of lists and classification indices for guiding users toward the books they might wish to order; including advertisements, the book comes to 760 pages. It is worth noting that this final catalogue is an outlier in some ways. The only twentieth-century example in the collection, it not only lists by far the largest number of fiction titles but also contains the largest proportion of never-before-listed works, as well as a surprising number of apparent rediscoveries, books which had appeared in previous catalogues but were subsequently delisted. It is unclear whether these represent an influx of new editions of old favourites, or the relisting (indeed, 'resurrection') of older books from storage in the library's cellars. Either way, it records a noticeable expansion of the library's fiction holdings around the turn of the twentieth century, at a time when the library was facing increasing competition from the growing public library system.

1.3.2 Additional Data

In some sections of this Element, I have used existing bibliographic datasets for comparative purposes. The most important of these has been Bassett's *At the Circulating Library: A Database of Victorian Fiction, 1837–1901*, an ongoing project which currently indexes 24,039 titles published during the nineteenth century. (This Element references the version of the data published in December 2023, which is referred to as Bassett 2024b or ATCL.) The digital bibliographic resources which were used for the earlier part of the century are *British Fiction 1800–1829* (Garside et al. 2004), and *The English Novel, 1830–1836* (Ebbes et al. 2016). These databases provide titles, author names and gender information (where available) and publication data. Together they provide a 'baseline' of published fiction throughout the nineteenth century for comparison against the combined Mudie's catalogues. While these bibliographies provide a substantive accounting of published nineteenth-century fiction, they are indicative rather than comprehensive. The three bibliographies define 'novels' differently and consequently employ slightly different inclusion criteria. The ATCL database is also an evolving collection, with titles continuing to be added; at the time of publication, it is estimated to be between 41 per cent and 72.4 per cent complete overall, with figures for multivolume fiction (two-, three-, and four-volume novels) more comprehensive than single-volume works (Bassett 2024a; personal communication). Because of this, some of the comparative analyses which are discussed here have focused on multivolume works rather than all published titles.

1.3.3 Missing Data

The combined Mudie's catalogues represent an important source of information on the library and the ways in which it served as a conduit – or barrier – between literature and the public. They are, however, an incomplete record, and they contain lacunae that should be borne in mind by anyone planning to use them as a historical source. As is likely evident from the description of the origins of this project, some of the limitations of the data which is discussed here arise as a result of the scope of the project and the resources available to the investigators, rather than to what is present in the historical sources.

The most obvious gap in this dataset is the absence of an account of the library's substantial non-fiction listings. A comprehensive survey of the library's holdings of non-fiction is outside of has been outside the scope of this project, but rough estimates based on page counts in our eight catalogues indicate that in terms of the number of titles, fiction represented less than half of what the library stocked in any given year, ranging from around 30 per cent to 42 per cent.[21] An estimate provided by C. E. Mudie himself

---

[21] Fiction pages in our catalogues comprise 30 per cent to 31 per cent of the 1848, 1857, and 1860 catalogues, and this proportion thereafter increases, reaching a peak of 42.4 per cent in 1885. The 1907 catalogue is not comparable due to differences in

in 1860 indicates that of the almost 400,000 volumes acquired in the preceding period of roughly two years, 57.7 per cent were non-fiction and 42.3 per cent were fiction (Mudie: 1860).[22] Numerically speaking, an analysis which does not examine Mudie's non-fiction is missing more than half of what the library circulated to its subscribers. Arguably, this poses a challenge to the understanding of what was considered vendible, or of the careers of the many writers working in the genres of history, biography, travel, sciences, and devotional literature. Any use of the combined Mudie's catalogue in its current form should take into consideration its status as a representation of a highly specific, if vibrant and culturally relevant, subsection of the whole.

The scope of the project that led to the creation of this dataset resulted in some unavoidable limitations. Although the library continued to function until 1937, the dataset currently ends with the 1907 catalogue, due to the focus of its parent project (VICTEUR) on the nineteenth century. Additionally, and for a variety of reasons, it is almost certain that some titles which were held by the library at some point will be missing from our dataset. As previously mentioned, not every surviving Mudie's catalogue has been included in this project, and it is possible that some books may have run their course during the inter-catalogue years and consequently not been captured in this survey. There is also evidence to suggest that the library itself refrained from advertising certain titles, despite their being held in stock. Both Keith and Colclough cite instances of novels being purchased by the library but not advertised in its catalogues due to concerns

formatting. Eliot (2009) generally observes similar proportions in fiction and non-fiction (despite a significant difference in page counts for the 1857 catalogue).

[22] The following list of the total number of works added since January, 1858, may interest your readers, as it indicates to some extent the relative circulation of various classes of works in the current literature: – History and Biography, 87,210 vols; Travel and Adventure, 50,572 vols; Fiction, 165,445 vols; Miscellaneous, including Works of Science and Religion, and the principal Reviews, 87,856 vols: total, 391,083 vols.(Mudie 1860: 451)
Mudie gives figures for volumes rather than titles, which is understandable for someone accustomed to considering the need for shelf space.

about their content, yet the works in question do appear in the combined catalogues somewhat after their initial publication date, perhaps to allow time for public debates to die down.[23] Colclough (2016) suggests that 'by the late 1860s, it was possible for subscribers to request some books that were not in the catalogue', a practice which was also in force in other contemporary libraries (44).[24] Fryckstedt suggests that rather than describing a work as not being held by the library, 'we should cautiously adopt "not listed by Mudie's" unless we can establish the truth by examining the publisher's archives' (Fryckstedt 1995: 27).

Records of the library's purchases of titles, and of borrowing by subscribers, are not available due to the absence of a surviving business archive for Mudie's. As previously mentioned, library borrowing records are rare before the nineteenth century.[25] Similarly, with a handful of exceptions, it is not possible to ascertain the number of volumes of each individual book that

---

[23] In a discussion of Rhoda Broughton's *Cometh Up as a Flower* (1867), Colclough (2016: 44) reports that despite an initial reluctance due to the work's 'frankness over sexual matters', Mudie's took 104 copies of its second impression, yet did not immediately list it in the catalogues. It did not appear in 1869 or 1871 (Fryckstedt 1995: 27); its earliest appearance in the combined catalogue is in 1876, but it then remained part of the library's collection until at least 1907. Describing the experience of 1859's *The Ordeal of Richard Feverel* in Mudie's, Keith quotes a letter from C. E. Mudie to its author George Meredith in which the librarian acknowledges buying 300 copies but withdrawing them from sale upon complaints from 'several respectable families'; the novel appears in the combined catalogues from 1885 onward (Keith 1973: 367).

[24] See Hiley 1992; Hammond 2006: 71–2.

[25] Kaufman's monograph *Borrowings from the Bristol Library 1773–1784*, Fergus's study of Samuel Clay's circulating library in Warwick, 1770–72, Gerrard and Weedon's discussions of working-class patrons of the Kidderminster Municipal Library and Huddersfield Female Educational Institute in 1855 and 1856, and Tim Dolin's study of the South Australian Library in Adelaide in the early 1860s provide accounts of some unusual survivals of borrowing records from before the twentieth century. Bassett's 2017 study of the Heath Book Club offers an intriguing perspective on a the practice of community book-borrowing outside the circulating library system.

were taken by the library.[26] From the catalogue data, we can (usually) pinpoint the times in which a book was available from the library, but not how many copies it held. As Mudie's correspondence with authors such as Charles Reade and James Payn demonstrates, this figure was of importance both to writers and to readers, and the two figures were interlinked: more borrowings of a novel meant larger orders for its author's next book, while an insufficient order by the library could be financially and reputationally devastating, as frustrated readers might give up trying to get access to a book.[27] As Section 4.3 shows, for authors, simply being represented in Mudie's catalogues by a large number of titles did not necessarily mean financial security.

In the absence of borrowing records for Mudie's and the other circulating libraries, the catalogues provide an invaluable source of information on the reading habits of the section of the public that could afford to subscribe. They do not, however, represent a faithful and complete record of what subscribers were reading, or even what works were accessible to them. Rather than assuming that the catalogues – which were available for purchase as well as for consultation in branches of the library – represent an accurate record of the library's holdings, it may be helpful to consider them as a part of its marketing apparatus. In his discussion of *Mudie's Library Circular*, a marketing periodical issued by the library which contained reviews and advertisements, Colclough (2016) argues that this text formed 'a vital part of an innovative strategy of audience control' (44) which was key to reviving the library's fortunes after its financial crisis of

---

[26] Finkelstein (1993) examined the library's orders from Bentley, Smith, Elder, John Murray, and Blackwood and Sons in the early 1860s. Griest provides many accounts of the library's subscription figures from letters and newspaper commentary. The business archives of W. H. Smith provide the most closely comparable record of a contemporary library (see Bassett 2020: chapter 4).

[27] Robert Browning cited Mudie's lack of copies as the direct cause of his giving up on Eliot's *Romola* (Griest 1970: 214). Charles Reade's correspondence with Mudie in the University of Illinois is almost entirely concerned with how many copies of his novels the library might take. Payn's experience is described in Section 2.1.

the early 1860s. The library's catalogues are also part of this strategy, if less visibly so. Their function was not to provide precise lists of what was available, but rather, what some scholars have termed 'vendible': works that were both appealing to potential and existing subscribers and which put forth what the library deemed to be the correct signals about what was appropriate reading for them (Kaufman 1967: 16; Joshi 2002: 51–68). As Broughton and Meredith's experiences indicate, a novel of debatable 'vendibility' might not be listed in a catalogue despite being available on request to some subscribers. Continued demand for certain works, particularly older novels, is also likely to have determined whether they were afforded space in the catalogue's main listings. Equally, the catalogues subtly draw extra attention to specific works that the library felt would be of interest to patrons, or that they wished to promote. They achieve this through the double-listing of titles by certain popular and/or prolific authors, both under their title and under their author's surname, which serves to render them more visible in much the same way as 'fronting' a book on a shelf in a modern bookshop. These strategies of concealment and revelation mean that the catalogues are not unbiased records of the library's holdings; rather, they provide evidence of the internal hierarchies that Mudie's perceived and perpetuated within their own collection.

2 Accession, Retention, and Delisting of Novels

'Many people imagine…that it pays us best to circulate inferior three-volume novels, and light literature generally, whereas the facts are entirely the other way. We like books that will read for six months or a year, and not lose their value in six weeks. In short, the best books are the best books for us.'

William Faux, quoted in *Publisher's Circular* (1891: 380)

2.1 Mudie's Economic Model

Almost from its opening and until at least the end of the nineteenth century, Mudie's maintained its position within the British publishing industry as one of the most important buyers and distributors of literature. As mentioned in Section 1, brand new fiction typically retailed at an artificially high price that discouraged direct sales to the public.[28] While some new fiction was made available through other means such as serialisation, and publishers occasionally experimented with cheaper first editions, most individuals who wanted to purchase a novel would wait until its publisher issued a second edition, usually in a considerably cheaper (inevitably one-volume) format. This would only occur, of course, if the first edition was sufficiently well reviewed and demanded by library patrons to tempt a publisher to bring out another edition, which was by no means guaranteed. An avid novel-reader's other option was to maintain a subscription to one of the major circulating libraries, in the understanding that this would provide them with early access to the latest fiction. For its part, Mudie's and major competitors maintained the supply of new works they needed to satisfy the reading public by purchasing copies in bulk directly from the publisher, generally at a steep discount (Griest 1970: 64–6).

In theory, subscribers got their hands on new novels from Mudie's in a manner similar to the way in which moviegoers attend the cinema today.

---

[28] While single-volume novels might retail at six shillings (or in some cases less), two-volume novels were generally priced at 21s and three-volume novels at 31s 6d.

In both cases, initial access was provided to the public on a mass basis by a central distributor, which in theory would satisfy the initial demand; later, an edition intended for home consumption would be released at an affordable price, and this could be purchased by those who had enjoyed the film or book upon its first release. In practice, this model only worked if the libraries had correctly estimated demand. Access to a very popular novel could prove elusive if the library had bought insufficient copies, and contemporary sources record numerous complaints on the topic both from disgruntled readers and worried writers. Mrs Humphry Ward's autobiography recounts her experience of sharing a train compartment with an excited reader who had just managed to acquire the first volume of Ward's latest novel, *Robert Elsmere*, from Mudie's, despite having been warned that it wouldn't be available for weeks.[29] The writer James Payn had a less gratifying experience of demand outstripping supply. After the publication of *What He Cost Her* (1877), he wrote apologetically to C. E. Mudie to express his concern that readers were reporting difficulty getting his novel through the library, and to ask if the library could rectify their underestimation of the demand for the book, 'the effect of which is to do me a serious injury' (Payn [c.1877]: 3). Meanwhile, Mudie's also had to attempt to maintain a delicate balance, ideally purchasing just enough copies to keep its subscribers satisfied. Overestimating the demand for a book could be a costly error, both in monetary terms and in terms of the space required to store unwanted copies of a novel. Multivolume works were particularly space-intensive; Arthur O. Mudie claimed that the appearance of a 6s edition of Mrs Humphry Ward's *Marcella* just three months after the library received its triple-decker copies resulted in Mudie's being left with '1,750 copies, or 5,250 volumes, of waste paper' (Griest 1970: 170),[30] while the failure of Disraeli's

---

[29] 'They told me no chance for weeks – not the slightest! Then – just as I was standing at the counter, who should come up but somebody bringing back the first volume. Of course it was promised to somebody else; but as I was there, I laid hands on it, and here it is!' (Ward 1918: 86–7; also quoted in Griest 1970).

[30] Throughout the nineteenth century, single-volume reprints of multivolume novels appeared ever more quickly and in greater numbers, as Eliot (1985) points out, rendering this issue increasingly urgent for the libraries.

Endymion resulted in 9,000 volumes for the library's catacombs (Nesta 2007: 64). The sale of second-hand books to the public was a key revenue stream for the library, and a rebinding department was maintained partly for this reason; as previously mentioned, bundles of books – in effect, miniature libraries – were sold off cheaply. This had the result that the buying decisions previously made by Mudie's had knock-on effects elsewhere within the industry. Hammond (2006) notes that some public libraries, despite having been ostensibly set up to provide a conduit for literature that was free from Mudie's supposed values, eventually took on a Mudie's subscription in order to ensure their readers had access to more obscure works that they could not otherwise provide (30). Meanwhile, the wholesale provision of second-hand copies of novels to smaller or more distant institutions – for example, the public libraries in Singapore (Atkin et al. 2019: 11) – extended the impact of the library's 'selection' policies far beyond its immediate circle of influence. Readers at the Singapore Public Library, like it or not, were largely choosing from novels that 'had already been preselected as appropriate for a middle-class family readership' in Victorian Britain (Wade and Fermanis 2023: 78).

Back at home, however, surplus second-hand fiction could not always be sold off to readers, and observers described the library's famous 'catacombs' (apparently C. E. Mudie's own term for them) as filled with shelves 'groaning' under the weight of no-longer-fashionable titles;[31] books in especially poor condition might meet with the worse fate of being recycled as fertiliser (Wynter 1861: 705; Preston 1894: 671–2). The constant need to clear space for new publications encouraged libraries to engage in a continual practice of winnowing, and this practice is reflected in the way in which the catalogues updated their listings over time. While Mudie's probably retained a few copies of even the most forgotten work against future need, the requirement to present its collection as up-to-date and

---

[31] C. E. Mudie argued that this phenomenon was part of what necessitated the library's 'selection' policies. 'No library could provide space for all the books that might be written, and as bad and stupid novels soon die and are worthless after death – no vaults could be found capacious enough to give them decent burial. The heavy cost of such unremunerative stock would also be greater than any purse could bear' (Mudie 1860: 451).

modern resulted in the disappearance of many titles from its catalogues as they ceased to be in broad demand, just as the physical copies of the books were sold off to whoever might take them. This continual state of renewal allows us to make inferences about the life cycle of works in the library and – to some extent – how the 'shelf lives' of works in Mudie's might impact upon the broader sphere of nineteenth-century fiction.

2.2 'Circulating Library Trash': Collection Items Published before 1842

In examining the selection of older novels which were made available by Mudie's, it becomes evident that the library prioritised the provision of recent fiction to its subscribers, and held (or at least, listed) very little older fiction: the bulk of the library's collection was built up year-on-year as new novels came out. Of course, the newest fiction was believed to be a key driver of subscriptions, but the sparseness of the library's selection of earlier novels – and the nature of the early works that *did* make it into the collection – is suggestive of an attempt to differentiate the library from earlier institutions, and to present an image of respectability and modernity to the public.

Commercial lending libraries providing 'books for hire' had been a feature of the British literary landscape since at least the early 1700s. Kaufman's detailed 1967 survey of British circulating libraries prior to 1800 identifies 112 such enterprises in London and 268 elsewhere (Kaufman 1967: 10). He highlights the size and diversity of these libraries' collections, and finds that their numbers increased steadily from the 1740s; quoting from a travel guide, he notes that by 1826, 'almost every small town in the kingdom possesse[d] its circulating library' (Britton 1826: 341). However, in the nineteenth and early twentieth centuries popular discourse tended to characterise such libraries as purveyors of reading materials (usually fiction) of an uninspired and unimproving kind. By 1842, when Mudie's officially went into business as a library, circulating libraries were widely viewed as 'both expensive and vulgar, providing access to novels without taste or morality' (Roberts 2006: 8). As one historian remarks, the proliferation of eighteenth-century circulating libraries, which occurred in tandem with increases in literacy rates and standards of living, was thought to have facilitated 'a great expansion of the reading public to include those who otherwise might not have been able to read or to afford books: servants, apprentices, and newly-leisured women, among others' (Fergus 1984: 166). As a consequence, libraries (alongside their readers and the reading materials they supplied) were frequently the subject of censure by satirists and moralists. Taylor (1943) characterises these views as comprising 'moral judgments imposed upon the novel by a middle-class conception of conduct and practical morality', coupled with fears that 'any wide reading by the lower orders [was] inconsistent with their life of manual labor' (Taylor 1943: 1).[32]

One of the most prominent and widely known of these institutions during the eighteenth century was William Lane's Circulating Library, also known as the Minerva Library, then 'incomparably the largest commercial lending library ... in existence' (Kaufman 1967: 15). From 1800 onward, the publishing arm of Lane's business, the Minerva Press, specialised in fiction and was famous for producing gothic novels; the Minerva Library, however, circulated a diverse selection of books, few of which were published by Lane, and most of which were non-fiction. Despite this, Griest and other modern scholars occasionally conflate the Minerva Press with the Minerva Library, and some nineteenth-century readers did the same.[33] In 1869, writer Francis Turner Palgrave addressed a personal letter to C. E. Mudie which illustrates this misconception:

> I recollect the era when 'circulating library trash' was the only
> term which was or could be applied to the publications com-
> posing the stock of such establishments. Of these miserable

---

[32] Fergus's survey of borrowing records in one provincial library registers some doubt over the extent to which book-borrowing in the eighteenth century contributed significantly to the general expansion in reading, noting that most customers were middle- or upper-class (Fergus 1984: 191)

[33] While Griest gives credit to Lane as a progenitor of many library franchises, she states that 'the popular taste for these tales of terror was being stimulated by William Lane's Minerva Press and by his circulating library in Leadenhall street' (Griest 1970: 10). Hudson's (2023) survey of the Minerva Press also characterises Lane's Library as a purveyor of novels rather than general literature (106, 207).

compositions the principal fountain was the 'Minerva Library'
or 'Lane's Library' in Leadenhall Street. The source which
flooded the land. Somewhat later, Hookham in Bond St began
to furnish a better article, but no marked progress was made
until you commenced business. And by affording the means to
the public and especially to the young the means of home
recreation the value of the instruction is vastly enhanced.

(Palgrave 1869: 2, 3)

Palgrave clearly intends to gratify his addressee by drawing a strong distinction between the Minerva and Mudie's library, characterising one as 'the
source which flooded the land' with the 'miserable compositions' produced by
the authors who wrote for the Minerva Press, while the other provides
wholesome 'home recreation' and instruction to the young.[34] In fact,
Kaufman's work on community libraries around the start of the nineteenth
century indicates that of over 20,000 titles listed by Lane's Library in its 1796–
1802 catalogue, less than 20 per cent of the total were fiction. Although the
Minerva Library was larger in scale than many of its contemporaries, and
more influential due to its business model of supplying works to smaller
regional libraries, this was not an atypical distribution. For all the London
libraries surveyed by Kaufman, non-fiction makes up a substantial portion of
their contents, with only Hookham's 1791 foreign-language catalogue offering more than 20 per cent fiction. This must have reflected demand from
subscribers; as Kaufman notes of the prevalence of non-fiction in most
catalogues, 'Booksellers continuing in business under whatever name do
not survive for a half-century or more (as a number of them did) without
knowing their business' (Kaufman 1967: 15). Contrary to beliefs such as those
expressed by Palgrave, Mudie's was not unique or innovative in its provision
of both fiction and non-fiction to the public; in fact, it made more novels
available to the public than the Minerva Library did.

---

[34] Palgrave's views on the quality and quantity of works issued by the Minerva
Press are strongly reminiscent of concerns relating to 'fictional proliferation' that
were prevalent in the early 1800s; see Hudson (2023).

Describing Lane's Library as 'by far the single most significant circulating library of the period 1740–1840', Jacobs notes that although by the 1820s it was no longer pre-eminent among the London libraries, the Leadenhall Street establishment was still in business until 1848 (Jacobs 2006: n.p.). At the time he established his own circulating library in 1842, C. E. Mudie would have been well aware of the reputation of the still-extant Minerva Library and its contemporaries, and in October 1860 he would declare to the *Athenaeum* that his desire had been to create a library that was distinctly different from what had gone before.

> I have always reserved the right of selection. The title under which my library was established nearly twenty years ago implies this: – the public know it, and subscribe accordingly and increasingly. They are evidently willing to have a barrier of some kind between themselves and the lower floods of literature.
>
> (Mudie 1860: 451)

Around the time he established his library – or perhaps more accurately, formalised the previously casual books-for-hire element of his stationery business – Mudie appears to have been at his choosiest about what constituted the 'lower floods of literature'. As Section 3 describes, the combined catalogues show that the proportion of all published works that Mudie's was willing to list in its catalogues increased steadily until at least the 1890s. Generally speaking, however, novels that were published before 1842 were at a distinct disadvantage compared against more modern titles, and this situation only intensified over time as older books were retired.

The earliest known Mudie's catalogue dates to the period 1848–9, appearing coincidentally at the same time the Minerva Library finally shut down. As Table 2 shows, in this catalogue (the shortest of the eight considered in this project), around a third of the library's listed novels date to the years between 1700 and 1842. In the later catalogues, both the percentage and number of titles from this pre-1842 cohort gradually decrease, reaching its nadir in 1885. The 1890s witness a slight resurgence

Table 2 Proportion of titles published between 1700 and 1842 which are listed in specific catalogue years.

	1848–9	1857	1860	1865	1876	1885	1895	1907
Titles, 1700–1842	275	273	252	211	145	128	145	175
All titles	797	1256	1428	2194	3526	4858	8392	15416
% of 1700–1842 in complete catalogue	34.5%	21.7%	17.6%	9.6%	4.1%	2.6%	1.7%	1.1%

in numbers, which may be due either to the rediscovery of old favourites in the 'catacombs', or to the publication of new editions.

Throughout the nineteenth century, a remarkably large proportion of the library's fiction dates to within its own lifetime. This situation may have been of benefit to writers whose careers were ongoing. However, in terms of representation, it placed prolific writers of the 1820s and 1830s at a comparative disadvantage. Several writers that Garside identifies as 'stalwarts' of this period, including Catherine George Ward, Hannah Maria Jones, Barbara Hofland, William Pitt Scargill, and the pseudonymous Rosalia St. Clair, are not represented in Mudie's at all (Garside 2013: 30).

In 1897, Mrs Alexander (Annie French Hector) noted this lack of representation in relation to the works of one early nineteenth century author, Caroline Norton, in the library:

> It is a curious instance of the change of fashion and the transient nature of popular memory that great difficulty is experienced in obtaining copies of Mrs Norton's works, especially of her poems. 'The Undying One', 'The Dream', and one or two smaller pieces, are found only in the British Museum Library. **The novels are embedded in the deeper strata of Mudie's, but are not mentioned in the catalogue of that all-embracing collection.** Yet forty years ago, Mrs. Norton acknowledged

that she made at one time about £1400 a year by her pen, this
chiefly by her contributions to the annuals of that time.

(Oliphant et al. 1897: 289; emphasis mine)

Mudie's in fact listed at least one of Norton's novels in all eight of the
catalogues in this study. However, a comparison of the works listed in
Garside and colleagues (2004) and Ebbes and colleagues (2016) published in
the 1830s against the combined Mudie's catalogue reveals titles by a number
of popular authors which would never find their way into a Mudie's
catalogue; these include works by G. P. R. James, John Galt, Lady
Charlotte Bury, Julia Pardoe, Horace Smith, Frances Eleanor Trollope,
and Catherine Gore. Journalist and novelist Harriet Martineau fared particularly poorly during this time period, publishing thirty-six fiction titles that
Mudie's never added to their collection.

While the early nineteenth century is poorly represented, the class of
fiction that is most notably absent from Mudie's is novels which predate
1800.[35] Just 22 listings from the combined catalogues (of over 20,000) are
for works of fiction published before 1800 (see Table 3). Of these, half
(including works by Fielding, Smollett, Sterne, and Richardson) don't
appear at all until 1907. Strikingly, between 1857 and 1885, just seven pre-
1800 titles are listed at all. These are William Beckford's *Vathek*;
Goldsmith's *Vicar of Wakefield*; Walpole's *Castle of Otranto*; Richardson's
Clarissa Harlowe; another edition of *Vathek* which is combined with *Otranto*
and M. G. Lewis's *Bravo of Venice*; Defoe's *Robinson Crusoe*; and Henry
Brooke's *The Fool of Quality*. Some of these are certainly nineteenth-
century editions: the combined *Vathek/Otranto/Bravo of Venice* was part
of Bentley's Standard Editions series and was first published in 1834, while
Robinson Crusoe (1719) and *The Fool of Quality* (1765–70) were republished
by Macmillan (1868) and Smith, Elder (1859) respectively.

It is tempting to conclude that the absence of some still-popular eighteenth-century writers from Mudie's was due to a loss of respectability by the

---

[35] The edition of the *Canterbury Tales*, which was published by the Lee sisters
between 1797 and 1805, is for the purposes of this work considered a nineteenth-
century text rather than a medieval one.

Table 3 Works in Mudie's combined catalogue which were published prior to 1800.

Title	Author	1848–9	1857	1860	1865	1876	1885	1895	1907	#catalogues
Adventures of Gil Blas	Le Sage, Alain René								1	1
Adventures of Joseph Andrews	Fielding, Henry								1	1
Clarissa Harlowe	Richardson, Samuel					1			1	2
Evelina	Burney, Frances		1						1	2
History of Amelia	Fielding, Henry								1	1
History of Sir Charles Grandison	Richardson, Samuel								1	1
Humphrey Clinker	Smollett, Tobias								1	1
Jonathan Wild	Fielding, Henry								1	1
Pamela	Richardson, Samuel								1	1
Peregrine Pickle	Smollett, Tobias								1	1
Robinson Crusoe, with Introduction by Henry Kingsley	Defoe, Daniel				1	1				2

Table 3 (Cont.)

Title	Author	1848–9	1857	1860	1865	1876	1885	1895	1907	#catalogues
Roderick Random	Smollett, Tobias								1	1
The Castle of Otranto	Walpole, Horace		1	1	1					3
The Life and Opinions of Tristram Shandy	Sterne, Laurence								1	1
The Vicar of Wakefield	Goldsmith, Oliver		1	1					1	4
Tom Jones	Fielding, Henry								1	1
Vathek	Beckford, William		1	1	1	1	1			6
Vathek; Castle of Otranto; and Bravo of Venice	Beckford, William; Walpole, Horace; Lewis, Matthew (trans)		1							1
Whole Works[1]	Defoe, Daniel	1								1
Whole Works	Smollett, Tobias	1								1
Whole Works	Sterne, Laurence	1								1

1. 'Whole Works' likely refers to collected editions; precisely which titles were included is unclear.

mid-Victorian period. The works of the novelist Samuel Richardson, which had a very belated debut in Mudie's, may represent a case in point. Richardson's *Pamela* (1740), now widely considered one of the first great English novels, does not appear in Mudie's at all until the twentieth century. His somewhat less controversial work *Clarissa* (1748) first appears in the 1876 catalogue, probably in an 1862 reissue by Tauchnitz. An 1818 reviewer for the *British Review* expressed the shift in attitudes towards these two works – both hugely popular in their day – when he remarked that 'by what unction of purity our great-grandmothers were preserved, when they studied *Pamela* without danger or disgust, we know not [. . .] *Clarissa* is less objectionable, though many of the scenes at Mrs. Sinclair's are such as are wholly unfit for modern ears'. The reviewer (possibly the writer Charles Maturin) emphasises a temporal demarcation between the book's original audience and its contemporary readers (or more accurately, listeners); what might have been considered acceptable reading material for the great-grandmothers of the readers of 1818 would not pass muster in the early nineteenth century (Maturin 1818: 40–1). It hardly needs to be stated that no novel published by Lane's Minerva Press appears in the nineteenth-century Mudie's catalogues considered here.[36]

By contrast, the persistence of Brooke's relatively obscure novel *The Fool of Quality* (1766–70) throughout the nineteenth-century catalogues suggests a more complex explanation. This eighty-year-old book did not by any means command the same popular appeal as *Robinson Crusoe*, or even *Pamela*, and one twentieth-century scholar described the rambling five-volume work as 'one of the worst novels ever written' (Allen 1955: 85). However, it retained some fans into the nineteenth century, including Coleridge, whose heavily annotated copy is preserved in the Huntingdon Library (Dike 1931). A new edition in two volumes was published by Smith, Elder in 1859, edited and enthusiastically introduced by Charles Kingsley; this is undoubtedly the same two-volume edition which appears

---

[36] Roche's *Children of the Abbey*, which appears in 1907, was originally published by Lane in 1796. Several British editions appeared in the later nineteenth century, of which the George Routledge & Sons edition of 1882 appears the likeliest candidate; some others were published in America.

in Mudie's catalogues in 1860, 1876, and 1885. Both Kingsley and his publisher had a long history with Mudie's. At least one of Kingsley's works can be found in every catalogue between 1849 and 1907, and most were retained indefinitely by the library once purchased. Finkelstein (1993) outlines the complicated financial interdependencies between Mudie's and the publishing houses that kept it stocked, noting that in the late 1850s Mudie's was Smith, Elder's best customer, buying between 30 per cent and 60 per cent of all stock the firm published in the years 1858–65; as Section 3.2 describes, an examination of published works in the combined catalogues found Smith, Elder to be tenth on the list of publishers who supplied novels to Mudie's in a sample of given years (as Table 7 demonstrates). Of this 1859 edition of *The Fool of Quality*, Finkelstein records that Mudie's bought up 250 copies, representing 35 per cent of the work's total sales (Finkelstein 1993: 41). It seems likely, therefore, that the presence of this book in the late nineteenth-century catalogues attests not so much to its continued appeal to Victorians a century after its first appearance – although the appearance of a new edition suggests that it was at least somewhat compatible with mid-nineteenth-century tastes – but rather to the strength of the business relationship between Mudie and one of its most closely linked publishing houses.

The best description of Mudie's patterns of acquisition, as they were laid down in its earliest days, is that the backbone of the library's collection was formed by the latest novels, to the exclusion of older favourites. As time went on, the appearance of a new edition might tempt the library to acquire an older work, especially if it were issued by a friendly publisher or prefaced by a writer with a known track record. However, titles that too closely resembled the cliched understanding of 'circulating library trash', that reminded patrons of the continued existence of Lane's Library a few miles away, or that simply represented the values of the eighteenth rather than the nineteenth century, were to be avoided at all costs: works like Roche's *Children of the Abbey* or Richardson's *Pamela* did not make a reappearance in the library until the beginning of the twentieth century. The library's purpose, of course, was not to maintain a historically representative collection but to build up a selection of novels that would appeal to subscribers of the current day, and its buying practices are no doubt the main reason for the relative absence of titles published prior to its establishment in 1842. As the next section will discuss, however, when such titles do appear in the combined catalogue, they are all the more notable.

2.3 The Persistence of Items in the Collection

Sales figures have rarely been reliable indicators of the popularity and reach of nineteenth-century novels. As McKitterick (2009) notes, 'books are not like other commodities' due to their ease of exchangeability (636). The availability of large numbers of (often lightly-used) second-hand copies of recently published novels have served to complicate understandings of public demand, both for contemporaries and modern scholarship. Library catalogues may seem little better on the face of it, given that they do not provide precise records of what customers *read*, only of what was made available to them. In his examination of the role of Mudie's library and its interactions with fiction as a commodity, Roberts (2006) pointed out that '[a] novel's exchangeability was overdetermined by many factors only obliquely related to its "content" or aesthetic value', which might include the library's relationships with its author and publishers, the size of the discount it could negotiate on a bulk order, and its perceived respectability (4). However, since the combined catalogues offer snapshots of the library at a number of different points in its history, they provide a perspective on the demand for specific works that is not readily available through other means. Shelf space was always at a premium in Mudie's, and with the sale of remaindered copies comprising an important element of the library's business, a work which was not in regular demand might find itself subject to removal. The appearance and disappearance of titles from the catalogues, then, are indicative of the demand that was perceived by those responsible for the day-to-day running of the library, and for compiling its catalogues.

In her consideration of accusations of censorship against Mudie's, Keith notes the presence of a number of works that are now generally considered canonical in the library's catalogues and surmises that 'if Mudie's can serve as an index of popularity, one might generalize from its history that selectivity is a good thing as long as the selection is intelligently made' (Keith 1973: 372). However, Keith's work is partly calculated to defend

Mudie against accusations of having stifled nineteenth-century literary creativity, and does not take into account the multitude of titles which faded into obscurity despite being listed in the catalogues. It remains difficult to say how many works of classic fiction were successful because of the library, or indeed, in spite of it. It is, however, possible to identify titles which were persistently made available to readers through the library, suggesting steady demand from its subscribers, and many of these titles are indeed familiar to readers in the twenty-first century.

Although the first decades of the nineteenth century are poorly represented in the combined catalogue, a small cohort of titles from prior to 1850 held their place on the library's shelves almost without a break. Out of the 20,000 novels in the dataset, 104 are found in every catalogue, which means that they were constantly available to readers throughout six decades under consideration. Familiar names dominate this list, with works by Walter Scott (25 titles), Edward Bulwer-Lytton (14 titles), James Fenimore Cooper (15 titles), Frederick Marryat (9 titles) and Charles Dickens (7 of his earlier works) accounting for two-thirds of the group. Present also are individual titles by authors who are well known now or were during the nineteenth century, including Jane Austen, W. M. Thackeray, Hans Christian Anderson, Nathaniel Hawthorne, Washington Irving, Charles Lever, Samuel Lover, Thomas Chandler Haliburton, G. P. R. James, William Harrison Ainsworth, and Benjamin Disraeli. The list also features some less familiar titles, however, suggesting that works such as Grace Aguilar's *Home Influence*, Annie Webb's *Naomi: Or, The Last Days of Jerusalem*, Albert Smith's *The Fortunes of the Scattergood Family*, and various novels by Elizabeth M. Sewell, might reward renewed scholarly consideration, having maintained their appeal to this specific portion of the reading public throughout the second half of the nineteenth century.[37]

[37] Aguilar and Webb's novels have been considered by modern scholarship largely in the context of representations of Jewishness and gender; Richa Dwor describes the inclusion of one of Aguilar's tales in an anthology of Victorian love stories as 'an almost unique instance of reading Aguilar's work in a context that is not explicitly concerned with gender, Judaism, or Anglo-Jewish history' (Dwor 2015: 86). Sewell's work has been primarily examined from the perspective of her

Another 95 titles can be found in 7 out of the eight catalogues (1857 onward), while an additional 159 titles appear in the catalogues from the 1860s and persist remain to the end of the century. As we add to this collection of highly persistent works with some of the slightly later catalogues, we find a number of the same authors' names appearing over and over again; in addition to Dickens, Lever, Ainsworth, Sewell, and Thackeray, we find Charlotte M. Yonge (13 persisting works), Dinah Mulock Craik and Anthony Trollope (11 works each), Margaret Oliphant (8 titles), Major George Whyte-Melville (8 titles) and sensation novelists Wilkie Collins (8 titles), Mrs Henry Wood and Mary Elizabeth Braddon (7 titles each). An additional 74 titles are represented in almost every catalogue, but with sporadic gaps and reappearances which are suggestive of irregularities in cataloguing rather than removal.[38] The resulting group of 432 novels, which are present in every catalogue from their first appearance until the end of the time period surveyed, may be considered perennial favourites, at least of the users – and compilers – of Mudie's catalogues. Their scarcity – they represent 1.96 per cent of all the fiction listed in the eight catalogues – is indicative of the dynamism of the library's acquisition and deaccession practices, and emphasises the degree of staying power which they represent.

This method of assessing popularity – persistence within the catalogues over time – has some drawbacks, not the least of which is that it fails to recognise the impact of titles published later in the century. As with all applications of the combined catalogue, the degree of demand for the texts is not explicit also unclear and appears to have varied significantly. It would seem natural that by the 1880s, for example, an old favourite from the 1820s such as

views on the education and reading practices of young women. Despite recently attracting some critical attention for his London novels and career as a mountaineer and performer, Albert Smith has been recently described as 'the most famous Victorian nobody has ever heard of' (McNee 2015: 7).

[38] The 1895 catalogue appears to be particularly prone to such lapses, with 187 titles disappearing after 1885 only to be reinstated in the 1907 catalogue. Among these is Stowe's *Uncle Tom's Cabin*, one of the best-selling novels in Britain during the nineteenth century (Altick 1957: 384); it seems highly unlikely that the library deliberately removed or delisted all of its copies.

Cooper's *Last of the Mohicans* or Scott's *Ivanhoe* would be seeing a different pattern of use than that of a recent work by a current novelist. However, direct evidence for reader demand is sparse and, where available, often unclear, even for titles as famous and widely available as Scott's novels.[39] What is evident is that the fact that Mudie's not only maintained copies of these titles in stock but actively advertised them in its lists indicates that they were considered a relevant part of the collection: either they had to be kept on hand to keep customers satisfied, or they in some way contributed to the library's concept of what a 'select' library needed to provide to its readers.

2.4 The Shelf Life of Novels and Authors in Mudie's

If Mudie's only retained around 2 per cent of the entire collection on an indefinite basis, then what was the experience of the other 98 per cent? An analysis of novel 'shelf lives', as represented by catalogue listings, indicates that in fact the most common experience for a novel is to appear in no more than two catalogues. If we look at the lifespans of novels over the course of the all eight catalogues, the most common scenario is for a novel to appear in just a single catalogue; for 12,750 titles, this is the case (see Table 4). However, this is a misleading figure, as the vast majority of these originate in the 1907 catalogue. As previously mentioned, this catalogue is an outlier in the collection, listing almost twice the number of fiction titles as the next most recent (and expansive) catalogue, 1895. Almost 10,000 of these appear for the first time in 1907, suggesting that between 1895 and 1907, the library underwent a significant expansion phase. This may have been coupled with an attempt to refresh the collection, since an unusually large proportion of the works which had appeared were present in 1895 were delisted at the same time.

---

[39] While the *Waverley* novels were printed in runs of tens of thousands upon their initial publication (Garside 2013: 22), a study of thirty southern hemisphere library catalogues from the 1820s to 1870s found that Scott's works, despite being almost universally present in these libraries, were rarely held in more than one copy, suggesting that subscriber demand for these books was steady but perhaps not extensive (Wade and Fermanis 2023: 87–8). Borrowing records from the South Australian Institute in the 1860s, however – an unusual survival for the nineteenth century – indicates that *Waverley* was the single most borrowed title between 1861 and 1862, being taken out 200 times by 130 subscribers (Dolin 2006: n.p.).

Table 4 Shelf lives of the 22,032 unique titles in the Mudie's fiction collection, measured in catalogue appearances.

Catalogue count	Number of titles
8 catalogues	104
7 catalogues	128
6 catalogues	132
5 catalogues	318
4 catalogues	927
3 catalogues	1953
2 catalogues	5720
1 catalogue (excluding 1907)	3259
1 catalogue (including 1907)	12750
1 catalogue (only 1907)	9491
Combined catalogues	22032

While the sudden appearance of 9,491 new titles at the end of the century is intriguing, it is not possible to say much more about these novels and how they fared into the twentieth century, since 1907 is the final catalogue in this survey. If we exclude this cohort, it transpires that in fact the most common experience of a novel in Mudie's was to appear in two catalogues before being delisted. While turnover was high, in general, three-quarters of all titles which were purchased by the library made it into at least a second of our catalogues before disappearing from the ranks. Although the time intervals between catalogues vary, the average shelf life of a Mudie's novel was around twelve years, assuming that it appeared in contiguous catalogues.[40] In the 1890s, William Faux of Smith's Library, Mudie's largest and most important competitor, estimated that their novels typically remained in circulation for just nine months, a figure that is remarkably

[40] This is the pattern for most titles novels, although some demonstrate gaps in their histories as a result of deliberate or accidental delisting, which could potentially have impacted the distribution of titles.

different from the pattern observed in the combined catalogues (Hiley 1992: 136). While the two commercial libraries were somewhat different, with railway bookstalls making up a crucial part of Smith's business model, they purchased from the same pool of available publications and supplied very similar groups of customers. We know from various accounts of the library and its 'catacombs' that Mudie's stored plenty of older titles in the long term. It is unclear whether they retained the 'long tail' of works as part of the strategy of representation previously described, or whether they were in fact still in demand – even on an occasional basis – by customers.

If we turn from the representation of *titles* to the representation of *authors* in the collection, we find that as before, there are just a small handful of privileged writers who are represented in every catalogue (see Table 5). Again, excluding the cohort of 1,907 first-timers (2,297 in total), we find that the most common lifespan for a nineteenth-century Mudie's author is two catalogues.

Table 5 Shelf lives of the 6,006 writers with works appearing in Mudie's fiction collection, measured in catalogue appearances.

Catalogue count	Number of authors
8 catalogues	31
7 catalogues	56
6 catalogues	80
5 catalogues	157
4 catalogues	253
3 catalogues	546
2 catalogues	1621
1 catalogue (excluding 1907)	965
1 catalogue (including 1907)	3262
1 catalogue (only 1907)	2297
All authors	6006
All authors (excluding new 1907)	3709

Metrics like these make it possible to identify authors whose popularity – at least, within the library – waxed and waned across the century. For example, a group of writers that are mentioned in every catalogue until 1885, only to then disappear, includes Mary Howitt, Lady Dacre, Lady Charlotte Bury, Horace Smith, Frederick Chamier, Emilie Carlén, and (perhaps surprisingly) Emily Brontë. A similar cohort, which peaks earlier and does not return after 1865, includes high-profile early nineteenth-century British writers Letitia Landon, Elizabeth Inchbald, George Henry Lewes, John Gibson Lockhart, and Professor John Wilson, as well as Irish writers John Banim and folklorist Thomas Crofton Croker. (Michael Banim, brother of John, lingers until the 1880s, represented by *The Town of the Cascades*.) It is notable that many of the writers in this latter category form part of a cohort sometimes referred to as the 'Fraserian Circle' for their association with the earlier days of *Fraser's Magazine*, an influential journal of the 1830s and 1840s. Some other prominent Fraserians, including its editor William Maginn, had already appeared in and cycled out of Mudie's catalogues by the 1850s; meanwhile, James Hogg's now-famous *Private Memoirs and Confessions of a Justified Sinner* (1824) would not appear until 1907, when the novels of fellow Fraserian and Scotsman John Galt also reappeared.[41] While *Fraser's* was financially successful and paid well for contributions, by the 1860s many of its former contributors had fallen upon hard times, as is attested by twenty-six applications to the Royal Literary Fund. Leary describes Thackeray and Carlyle, the two most prominent and successful Fraserians, as untypical of the group (Leary 1994: 113); works by both men appeared in Mudie's throughout the nineteenth century.[42] In the case of this particular

---

[41] Almost all of Galt's older works resurface in 1907, having disappeared from 1865 onward; this may be explained by Blackwood's issuing a collected edition of his works in 1895. Hogg's work was reissued in 1894 by J. Shiells and Co. with the title *The Suicide's Grave, Being the Private Memoirs and Confessions of a Justified Sinner*, and this is almost certainly the version which appears in Mudie's 1907 catalogue (as *The Suicide's Grave*). Both authors had died six decades previously, Galt in 1839 and Hogg in 1835.

[42] Carlyle's *Goethe's Wilhelm Meister* was listed as fiction in the 1848 catalogue and thereafter was featured alongside the rest of his works in the non-fiction section.

literary network, it appears that representation in Mudie's catalogues was surprisingly closely correlated with real-life fortune.

The permanent disappearance of any title or author from the combined catalogue is relatively uncomplicated, but cases in which a title or author reappears after an interval prompt additional questions about book survival and changing trends. Around fifty novelists experience gaps of two or more catalogues before reappearing. In some cases, as we have seen, the reinstatement of an old favourite in the catalogues probably occurs at the appearance of a new edition: for example, the publication of Routledge's 1893 'Longford Edition' of Maria Edgeworth's *Collected Works* is the likeliest explanation for her reappearance in the 1895 and 1907 catalogues after a substantial gap in the middle of the century. New editions, which appeared in the 1880s, of Frances Burney's *Evelina* (1778) and Richard Cobbold's *Margaret Catchpole* (1845) also appear to explain their revival in the catalogues, while George Croly's *Salathiel* (1828), which was reprinted in the 1890s, appeared in 1907 after a gap of three catalogues. (His other work, *Marston* (1846), was neither reprinted nor reinstated.) In many of these cases, simple wear and tear is likely to explain the sustained absence of a book from the catalogues, especially once its age or scarcity had made it difficult to replace. Colclough's discussion of the destruction of books in the Victorian era argues that the eventual demise of a library book at the hands of subscribers was not necessarily seen as a bad thing, with 'dirt, grease, and destruction' viewed as 'signs of a satisfied mass audience': 'That books become 'exhausted', or are 'read to death' during this process is thus seen by an author writing for a periodical text aimed at a mass audience as evidence of the successful turning of the machine of circulation' (Colclough 2014: 146).

It is likely that wear and tear contributed to the disappearance of some still-valued titles from the combined catalogue, but evidence for the cause of a book's disappearance or reappearance is generally scarce. However, one author left a personal record of a chequered history with the library. James McGrigor Allan's three-volume novel *Ernest Basil* (1857) was listed in catalogues in 1857, 1860, and 1865. However, after that date, the novel disappeared, and McGrigor Allan's subsequent four books are not found in any of the catalogues. McGrigor Allan's own version of these events can be found in the records of the Royal Literary Fund, which he applied to (successfully) in both 1866 and 1869. While Allan's account is certainly hostile towards Mudie's, referring to Charles Edward as 'that self-appointed Literary Dictator', it provides a fascinating insight into the interactions between writers and the library's selection processes. His 1866 Royal Literary Fund application form alleges that his most recent work, *Father Stirling*, was personally rejected by Mudie with the justification that the subject was unsuitable for a novel. Also included in the application is an open letter to C. E. Mudie which McGrigor had printed and circulated to the periodicals, which claims that Mudie had informed him 'that if I would write a novel which could be put into the hands of young people you would circulate it, and make some compensation for the rejection of four of my books'. Following the publication of this letter, *Ernest Basil* was listed one final time, in the 1865 catalogue, but after that it disappeared from the library's catalogues. McGrigor Allan (who also worked as a portrait painter) would not publish another book until *The Wild Curate* in 1887; perhaps surprisingly, this novel (and one more, in 1907) seems to have been taken by the library without issue. As the following chapter will describe, the later decades of the nineteenth century would witness some changes in the library's selection policies.

3 Selection in Practice: A Ten-Year Sample of Published Novels and Their Shelf Lives

My dear sir,

Can you make room for one more novel on the shelf which you have already permitted me to encroach upon?

Amelia B. Edwards to C. E. Mudie, 22 November 1865

3.1 Overall Numbers

The precise nature of Mudie's 'selection' policies – the protocols dictating which books the library would purchase, and at what rates – has been a contested topic since the early years of the library. For many nineteenth-century authors, the difficulty of determining exactly what factors would lead to the exclusion of their novels from Mudie's was a cause of frustration. The library's presumed preference for three-volume novels was irksome, as many pointed out,[43] but at least this requirement was clearly defined. However, despite C. E. Mudie's own claim that the 'moral reasons' which dictated the library's selection process were 'obvious' (Mudie 1860), they were not always apparent to novelists. George Moore's prolonged dispute with the library represents the most well-known and public challenge to Mudie's 'selection', but he was not the only writer who felt that the library's accession policies were ill-defined, prejudicial, and antithetical to freedom of artistic expression. McGrigor Allan's description of his experience with his 1864 novel *Father Stirling* demonstrates the difficulty inherent in attempting to break new topical or stylistic ground. In his application to the Royal Literary Fund, he describes this work (on 'the evils of priestly celibacy') as having been 'written in a grave impartial spirit' and with the public good in mind, and notes his vexation at being personally informed by Mudie that it was unsuitable (McGrigor Allan 1866). Conversely, some novels that featured controversial content were accepted into the library without hesitation.

---

[43] Griest (1970) provides numerous testimonials to the difficulty of filling (or restricting oneself to) the 1,000 pages required for three volumes, from writers including Charles Reade, Israel Zangwill, Elizabeth Gaskell, Rhoda Broughton, George Gissing, Anthony Trollope, Frances Eleanor Trollope, and Charlotte Brontë (89–100).

Colclough's work on sensation fiction notes that *Aurora Floyd*, one of several sensation novels which Mudie's enthusiastically promoted, contained scenes and topics that were described by reviewers as 'bad in taste' and 'bad in morals' (Rae 1865: 180, quoted by Colclough 2016: 44), and the library's shifting goalposts for respectability did not go unnoticed by contemporaries, some of whom publicly accused the library (and Mudie himself) of hypocrisy. George Moore's pamphlet *Literature at Nurse*, which he published after several rejections from Mudie's, helpfully provides synopses and excerpts from a number of Mudie's novels by Mrs Campbell Praed, W. H. Mallock, Robert Buchanan, and Ouida, which as he accurately observes, depict violence, murder, seduction, adultery, and (worst of all) obscene photographs. One contemporary critic, cited by Katz, went so far as to argue that 'moral and literary selection' was merely a smokescreen to conceal purchasing decisions of a purely economic nature: 'Mudie "will not touch a book he cannot buy at half-price", and when readers inquire after one such book, Mudie's employees tell them "[i]t isn't a proper book"' (Katz 2017: 404). The availability of large-scale longitudinal data on Mudie's library holdings, in addition to expansive bibliographic records for the nineteenth century, has made it possible to gather some indication of precisely what the library was buying, and how representative this was of what was being published at the time. It has not been practicable to compare the library's holdings against *all* the novels that are known to have been published while it was active. However, for a sample of ten discrete years, publication data from ATCL has been compared against the combined catalogue, in order to determine which and how many of the year's novels found their way into Mudie's.

This study focuses first on a cluster of years immediately after the library's establishment in 1842, and then examines roughly one year from each decade thereafter, generally dated to two years prior to the Mudie's catalogues that have been indexed by the larger study.[44] The latest year in this sample, 1899, was chosen in order to examine the outcome of the much-discussed 'death of

---

[44] This time period was chosen in order to allow as many works as possible to have appeared in the catalogue. By the time the 1876 catalogue was printed, for example, a novel published in 1874 would have had two years to be absorbed into the library's collection (taking any delays into account), and was unlikely to have been deaccessioned.

the triple-decker' following an edict issued jointly by Mudie's and Smith's libraries in June 1894, which specified the maximum price per volume that the library would be willing to pay going forward, and requesting a moratorium on cheap second editions being issued less than a year from first publication.[45] For each year under consideration, every title published in that year (listed in Bassett 2024b) was manually checked against the combined Mudie's catalogue, to identify if it was ever listed. The publishing data illustrates the significant rate of expansion in fiction publishing between the 1840s and 1890s: the number of novels published in the first year under consideration, 1842, was just 92, but by the end of the century this figure had risen to 684. Comparing these titles against the combined Mudie's catalogues (see Table 6) makes it clear that although the library's expansion occurred in tandem with the broader fiction landscape, the proportion of published novels that it accepted increased as time went on.

Of the cohort of novels that were published in 1845, three years before the appearance of Mudie's first surviving catalogue, only 43 per cent find a place in the combined catalogues. By 1899, 74.9 per cent of all published fiction titles were appearing in Mudie's at some point. While a degree of change is to be expected in the running of any institution over a fifty-year span, it is still notable that, by the end of the century, what Mudie had in 1863 termed the 'lower floods of literature' – then presumably around half of all works – had fallen to a quarter.

While the rate of acceptance follows a general upward trend as time goes on, there is a degree of variation from year to year that is likely related to events in the history of Mudie's. The temporary rise in acceptance rates that can be seen in the late 1850s coincides with the library's move to larger premises. At this time, Mudie's was acquiring books at an unprecedented rate,[46] partly in order to populate its new building and partly because it was

---

[45] For a detailed history of this event and its effects, see Griest 1970, chapters 7 and 8 ('The Collapse' and 'The End of the Triple-Decker'); see also Bassett 2020, chapters 4 and 5.

[46] Finkelstein (1993) notes that of the almost 960,000 volumes acquired by Mudie's between 1858 and 1862, 'well over 391,000 of these volumes were acquired between January 1858 and October 1859' (22). As Figure 1 indicates, between

Table 6 Novels accepted by Mudie's, as a percentage of all fiction titles published in a ten-year sample.

Year	All published novels	No. in Mudie's	Percentage listed in Mudie's
1842	91	22	24.20%
1845	116	50	43.10%
1852	162	60	37.00%
1855	154	85	55.20%
1858	192	118	61.50%
1863	348	171	49.10%
1874	451	225	49.90%
1883*	427	285	66.70%
1893*	586	425	72.50%
1899*	685	512	74.70%

in the midst of a book-buying arms race with an aggressive competitor. Publisher William Tinsley would later recall that the rivalry between Mudie's and the newly formed Library Company Limited resulted in 'phenomenal sales that had not been heard of before that time, or since' (Tinsley 1900: 60). This buying frenzy, which appears to have prompted a relaxation in selection standards, placed the library in a precarious financial position which necessitated the imposition of austerity measures. As Finkelstein describes in 'The Secret', during the period immediately following these events, when the library was attempting to recover from its financial instability, the size of the library's orders from specific publishers shrank dramatically (Finkelstein 1993: 37). This phenomenon can also be

1857 and 1865, the library's fiction collection almost doubled (from 1,257 to 2,198 titles).

observed in our data from 1863, which sees Mudie's acceptance rates drop
back below 50 per cent for the first time in a decade.

While the library had been gradually moving toward a more capacious
concept of acceptability in fiction over its first few decades, the percentage of
novels acquired took a particularly notable leap between 1876 and 1885 from
under 50 per cent to almost 67 per cent. This increase coincides with an event in
the Mudie family that had significant implications for the running of the library.
Upon the death in 1879 of the presumptive heir of the company, Charles Henry
Mudie, his father Charles Edward was devastated, and the business fell into
a degree of disarray that was felt elsewhere in the publishing industry.[47] By
around 1884, Charles Edward Mudie was largely retired, and had passed on
the day-to-day running of the library to his son Arthur O. Mudie and
a nephew.[48]

It had long been a commonplace to treat Mudie the librarian as equiva-
lent to Mudie's the library. Novels from 1861's *The World's Furniture*
('What a luxury the existence of Mudie is! I think he deserves a statue
being raised in his honour') to 1895's *The Comedy of Cecilia* ('[A]ll I had to
read was what Mudie chose to send down') make tongue-in-cheek references to the library as an individual, and the same tendency can be observed
throughout the work of Griest and other historians.[49] During his lifetime,

---

[47] Griest (1970) quotes an 1880 letter from James Payn stating that the staff of
Smith, Elder 'complain bitterly of Mudie's absence affecting his orders' (26).

[48] [H]e was broken down [. . .] by the shock of losing his eldest son, Charles,
a young man of great promise, who had been associated with him in the
management of the business, and to whom he was very tenderly attached. Since
then the management of affairs has been in the hands of Mr. Arthur O. Mudie, his
surviving son, and of Mr. Kingsford Pawling, a nephew of the late Mr. Mudie.
(Preston 1894: 670)

[49] Keith's (1973) 'Literary Censorship and Mudie's Library' is couched as a personal
defence of the head librarian in his (presumed) role as censor, arguing that '[it]
was not Mudie who victimized the public, but the public who victimized Mudie'
(371). Roberts (2006) uses 'Mudie' as a convenient shorthand for the management
of the library in statements such as 'Mudie's concern over the percentage of his
discount could often determine if a novel would be purchased at all' (3), as does
Shattock (2012) in statements such as '[it] was virtually impossible for a novel to

C. E. Mudie endorsed and encouraged this personification through statements such as his assertion to the *Athenaeum* that 'I have always reserved the right of selection' (Mudie 1860), implying that even if he did not personally read all 900 pages of every novel that was published, he at least had a good idea of what they were about. Yet the notion that a single individual could serve as an overseer, manager, and reader is rendered unrealistic by the sheer scale of the business in its later years, not to mention the length of the average Victorian novel. The actual process of choosing, screening, and vetoing items for the library's collection, typically construed as belonging to Mudie in his role as omniscient Victorian patriarch, must surely have been undertaken by multiple staff members. However, the change in acceptance rates which coincides with the transition to new management is noticeable, and suggests both that C. E. Mudie's management was indeed very hands-on, and – as the next section will outline – that Arthur O. Mudie and his colleagues had a rather different conception of the nature and purpose of 'selection'.

3.2 Publishers and Format

As our sample of ten years of published fiction in Mudie's indicates, the proportion of published novels which were accepted by the library had reached almost 67 per cent by the early 1880s and would only increase in subsequent years. The complete sample of over 3,000 published novels is too large to allow for easy conclusions about which genres and topics were most (or least) acceptable to the library. However, since Bassett's ATCL database includes information on the publisher, place of publication, and length (in volumes) of each work, it is possible to make some inferences about how these factors influenced the likelihood of a novel being accepted by the library.

Within the ten individual years in our sample, Bassett (2024b) identifies 3,208 novels which were brought out by 298 named publishers. (Six

succeed without a subscription from Mudie' (7). Throughout Griest's (1970) monograph, 'Mudie' is used as a stand-in for the library's management; see for example the discussion of the firm's dealings with Blackwood (179).

titles have no place or publisher specified). From this cohort, Mudie's acquired and listed just over 61 per cent of the total, from 176 publishers. When we examine this group of 1,962 novels, it becomes evident that the majority of the fictional works that Mudie's acquired came from firms that had a strong track record of sales to the library. Of the books acquired, 86.6 per cent (1,699) come from firms who all sold the library ten or more titles during the sample years (54 publishers in total). A core group of 11 high-output publishers each provided the library with 60 or more titles during the years in question: the 880 novels from these 11 firms comprise just under 45 per cent of all the fiction that Mudie's accepted during these years (see Table 7). However, a novel's acceptance into Mudie's was not solely determined by its publisher. The library rarely took everything that was published by any given firm; even its three most reliable suppliers (Hurst and Blackett, Bentley, and F. V. White) occasionally published titles that are not found in the combined catalogue.[50] Some small publishers, such as Bradbury and Evans, Kegan Paul, and George Bell and Sons, managed to sell all of the five or six titles that they published during these years to Mudie's. Meanwhile, a couple of the most prolific publishers were largely snubbed by the library. Mudie's seemingly had little appetite for the titles published by the SPCK (Society for Promoting Christian Knowledge) or the RTS (Religious Tract Society), listing just 18.3 per cent and 6.7 per cent of their publications from these years respectively. Bassett identifies the kind of novels that these firms produced – usually short, inexpensive, and of a moral or religious persuasion – as less prestigious than the works Mudie's generally carried; the titles from SPCK and RTS which do appear in Mudie's appear to be primarily naval- and adventure-themed (Bassett 2020: 183).

---

[50] In some cases, the absence of a book from the combined catalogue may in fact indicate a publisher declining to sell a title to Mudie's. Publishers sometimes pushed back against the library's demands for discounted rates; a note in Richard Bentley's handwriting, on a request from Mudie's for a reduction in the wholesale price of a novel from 15s to 12s, reads 'We can sell out probably all at 18/- elsewhere' (Griest 1970: 65).

Table 7 Publishers who supplied more than sixty novels to Mudie's in the ten-year sample.

Publisher	Titles listed by Mudie's	Titles not listed by Mudie's	All titles	% listed
London: Hurst and Blackett	147	8	155	94.80%
London: Bentley	109	36	145	75.20%
London: F. V. White	98	4	102	96.10%
London: Chatto and Windus	79	8	87	90.80%
London: Chapman and Hall	67	6	73	91.80%
London: Macmillan	66	3	69	95.70%
London: Tinsley Brothers	66	6	72	91.70%
London: Sampson Low	64	19	83	77.10%
London: T. C. Newby	63	40	103	61.20%
London: Smith, Elder	61	9	70	87.10%
London: Hutchinson	60	1	61	98.40%
All titles from these eleven publishers	880	140	1020	86.30%
All titles from 298 publishers in ten-year sample	1962	1246	3208	61.20%

In his 1860 letter to the *Athenaeum*, C. E. Mudie referred readers to 'my lists of books in circulation' as proof of 'the inclusive character of the collection, and of the absence of all sectarian or party bias'. If we take the representation of works from different publishers into account, this statement appears reasonably well supported. Although the output of a number of large firms dominates the combined catalogue, it was still possible for works by smaller publishers, outside of the mainstream, to make their way to readers via Mudie's shelves. However, when we turn to the information on volumes, another narrative emerges.

As Table 8 indicates, for novels published in any number of volumes during the library's first decade (1842 to 1852), acceptance levels are consistent with C. E. Mudie's assertion that the library was choosy about what it acquired for its fiction collection. For example, in 1852, we see acceptance rates hovering around 40 per cent for single-, double-, *and* triple-decker novels, suggesting that selection policies were being applied in a roughly even-handed way; multivolume novels published in 1852 held a minimal advantage over their one-volume peers. By 1855 this situation had changed dramatically. Just under a third of all single-volume novels, which were numerically the largest group, were acquired by the library. By contrast, the vast majority of all works which were published in two or three volumes – a minimum of 80 per cent in all years from 1855 to 1893 – are listed in at least one Mudie's catalogue. Triple-deckers were at an even greater advantage: at least 90 per cent of all three-volume novels published in the sample years was acquired by the library. By the start of the 1890s, any three-volume novel was almost guaranteed a place on Mudie's shelves, with almost 98 per cent of all triple-deckers published in 1893 appearing in the combined catalogue.

As Griest's work demonstrates, commentators have long recognised that triple-deckers were the preferred format for Mudie's, and although some single-volume novels were present in the library, they were more likely to be excluded.[51] However, it has generally been assumed that the library's much-discussed 'selection' criteria were also applied to three-volume novels, and that length was just one of the facets under consideration when the library placed its orders. What these figures suggest is that little 'selection', if any, could have been applied to multivolume novels after 1855. The triple-decker really was king, and two-volume novels were only slightly less acceptable.

[51] See, for example, chapter 3, 'Mudie's and the Three-Decker' (Griest 1970: 35–57).

Table 8 One-, two-, and three-volume novels from the ten-year sample, acceptance rates in Mudie's.[1]

Year	Novels accepted by Mudie's			All published			% Accepted by Mudie's		
	1 vol	2 vols	3 vols	1 vol	2 vols	3 vols	1 vol	2 vols	3 vols
1842	6	4	12	26	10	55	23.1%	40.0%	21.8%
1845	14	9	29	36	18	62	38.9%	50.0%	46.8%
1852	29	9	24	77	21	60	37.7%	42.9%	40.0%
1855	29	11	45	91	13	50	31.9%	84.6%	90.0%
1858	45	30	43	111	36	45	40.5%	83.3%	95.6%
1863	59	37	75	225	46	77	26.2%	80.4%	97.4%
1874	83	36	106	294	45	112	28.2%	80.0%	94.6%
1883*	97	38	151	218	46	163	44.5%	82.6%	92.6%
1893*	252	49	129	401	53	132	62.8%	92.5%	97.7%
1899*	511	0	0	685	0	0	74.6%		
Total	1125	223	614	2164	288	756	52.0%	77.4%	81.2%

[1] The ATCL data for single-volume novels is incomplete after 1880, which means that figures for single-volume novels may be inaccurate for the years marked with asterisks. Data for multivolume novels is robust.

The lively public discussion surrounding the exclusion of specific books from the library, such as Arthur Robins's *Miriam May* (1860), Annie Edwards's *The Morals of May Fair* (1858), and several of George Moore's novels, has often been taken as evidence that Mudie's strictures on taste and morality were of paramount importance in determining its acquisition policies, a perception which was no doubt to the library's liking. However, it is probably the rarity of such exclusions that heightened the impression they made on the public. When George Meredith's three-volume *The Ordeal of Richard Feverel* was published in 1859, he could reasonably have expected it to be welcomed by Mudie's, as had occurred with 96 per cent of the previous year's published triple-deckers. On discovering that the library would no longer advertise the 300 copies of his novel that it had purchased, he expressed his irritation in a letter to Samuel Lucas: 'I find I have offended Mudie and the British Matron. He will not, or haply, dare not put me in his advertised catalogue. Because of the immoralities I depict! O canting Age!' (George Meredith to Samuel Lucas, 1859, in Lindsay 1956: 94). In attributing the cause of his rejection to having offended 'the British Matron', Meredith anticipates the 'two ladies from the country' that allegedly objected to George Moore's *A Modern Lover* over twenty years later (Moore 1976: 30–1), but interestingly, Mudie's original description of those who had objected to *Richard Feverel* appears to have been the less gender-specific phrase 'several respectable families'; on another occasion, he requested that an author submit a novel that could be put into the hands of 'young people' (Lounger at the Clubs 1864: 7). As Section 4.5.3 will discuss in more detail, contemporary discourse relating to library censorship was frequently gendered, coalescing around two imagined female figures: one whose perceived vulnerability was posited as the reason for 'selection' (the 'Young Girl'), and one whose zeal for enforcing 'selection' was viewed as second only to Mudie himself (the 'British Matron'). Griest's (1970) chapter 'The British Matron and the Young Girl' accepts these constructions as arising inevitably from the Victorian family structure, stating that the practice of reading aloud meant that 'it was only natural that the standards were established for younger members of the audience, especially girls' (137); despite the title, she does not make any reference to the role of the matron in this dynamic. Yet the question of whether the British reading public needed, demanded or even just welcomed the library's role of protective 'barrier' against the 'lower floods of literature' is immaterial if it in fact exercised only the most minimal 'selection' upon the type of novel which was widely believed to be its specialty.

4 Cents and Censorship: Representation in Mudie's and Its Impacts

4.1 Single-Volume and Multivolume Novels in Mudie's Catalogues

While the earliest and latest catalogues in this survey (1848–9 and 1907) do not include volume information in their fiction listings, the six catalogues published between 1857 and 1895 do supply this data.[52] Using the combined catalogues, therefore, it has been possible to build up a picture of the representation of single-, double-, and triple-decker novels in Mudie's collection, and to examine how this compares against the broader publishing landscape. Broadly speaking, Mudie's fiction collection kept pace with trends which have been identified in modern scholarship on publishing in the nineteenth century. According to Bassett's extensive bibliographic survey of nineteenth-century fiction, multivolume novels maintained a consistent market share (generally comprising a third of all new fiction) from the late 1830s until the 1870s, with a peak in production occurring in the 1880s which saw multivolume fiction rise to more than half of all published novels. Numbers fell dramatically in the early 1890s, but the libraries' 1894 declaration in favour of single-volume novels did not immediately kill off multivolume works, which instead 'linger[ed] on in decline for another four years' (Bassett 2020: 31).

As Table 9 shows, single-volume novels dominate every catalogue in this study, comprising more than half the collection in every year except for 1876 and 1885.[53] Bassett has argued that in general, 'the three-volume novel enjoyed

---

[52] A novel which appears in two, three, or more volumes is generally marked as such in its listing. Single-volume novels are not usually specifically indicated in the catalogues, but we have inferred that any work not described as multivolume is present in a single-volume edition, and spot-checking indicates that this is accurate.

[53] In each catalogue, a small percentage of single-volume titles in each catalogue were described in the previous catalogue as two- or three-volume; this cohort ranges from 2.3 per cent (1865) to 6.4 per cent (1885) of single-volume titles. The reason for these changes is not known but may be due to the replacement of titles with newly published single-volume editions, irregularities in cataloguing, or possibly the rebinding of multiple volumes together.

Table 9 Overall percentage of works listed in Mudie's catalogues, by volume.

Volumes	Number of titles in the catalogues							Percentage of titles in the catalogues						
	1857	1860	1865	1876	1885	1895		1857	1860	1865	1876	1885	1895	
1	786	838	1099	1490	2220	4979		62.6%	58.7%	50.1%	42.3%	45.7%	59.3%	
2	170	212	394	633	730	988		13.5%	14.8%	18.0%	18.0%	15.0%	11.8%	
3	289	367	689	1392	1899	2415		23.0%	25.7%	31.4%	39.5%	39.1%	28.8%	
Other formats (4 to 36 volume editions)	11	11	12	11	9	10		0.9%	0.8%	0.5%	0.3%	0.2%	0.1%	
Total	1256	1428	2194	3526	4858	8392								

its greatest moment in the 1870s and 1880s' (Bassett 2020: 31), and this was also the case within Mudie's. In the combined catalogues, the high point for the triple-decker occurs in 1876 (39.5 per cent) and 1885 (39.1 per cent); in all other years, single-volume novels represent more than half the fiction collection, and they are always the most numerous. (Two-volume novels range from 11.8 per cent to 18 per cent of the collection, peaking in 1865 and 1876.[54]) A year after the libraries' declaration against multivolume novels, single-volume works were clearly on the ascendant, having grown from 46 per cent of the collection in 1885, to just under 60 per cent in 1895.

The fact that Mudie's held a substantial proportion of single-volume novels has been recognised by prior studies, most notably by Eliot, who found that the prevalence of one-volume novels (at never less than 44 per cent of the total, by his count) in Mudie's is directly contradictory of claims such as Coustillas's statement, 'They [the circulating libraries] would not hear of one-volume fiction – an open threat to their monopoly' (Eliot 2009: 37).[55] One-volume novels, rather than being taboo, were the backbone of the library's collection. Yet, substantial evidence exists of authors such as Elizabeth Gaskell, George Gissing, Rhoda Broughton, and Francis Eleanor Trollope, among others, who were convinced to add additional material to their novels or who lost money by failing to do so; in 'Novelists, Novels, and the Establishment' Griest writes that 'as long as the three-decker was in power ... chapters continued to be added by authors who could not fill its pages' (Griest 1970: 94–101). What appears to be lost in this argument is a distinction between the preferences of the publishers (who were the ones actually requesting the extensions to the novels) and the libraries, who had tired of the triple-decker long before 1894.[56]

---

[54] Just a handful of novels in four or more volumes are ever listed, including Eliot's *Daniel Deronda* and *Middlemarch*, Edgeworth's *Tales of Fashionable Life*, Trollope's *The Prime Minister*, and several titles by Bulwer-Lytton. Such long works were liable to be replaced by sets of fewer volumes in Mudie's later catalogues.

[55] While Eliot's method and the specific catalogues he examined are slightly different to mine, our findings are broadly in agreement.

[56] In July 1894, Arthur O. Mudie asserted in a letter to Richard Bentley that he had long-standing personal and professional objections to three-volume novels

If Griest's conclusion that the libraries encouraged the production of triple-deckers by 'making publishers ... unwilling to settle for fewer [volumes]' is not supported by the actual numbers that they purchased, her other arguments in favour of three-volume novels are more persuasive. Griest and others have argued that writers made a better living from longer works, which (usually) commanded higher purchase prices from publishers.[57] Griest also suggests that single-volume novels held less prestige, arguing that they were typically viewed as insubstantial, often poor-quality works: 'light, charming perhaps, but often questionable'. Quoting a publisher's letter to the *Daily News* in 1871, she states that an attempt by an unknown author to publish in one volume would be viewed as 'sheer folly': 'The trade would fight shy of him, the public would not buy him, and the press would inevitably snub him.' Almost as an aside, Griest also notes that the exceptions to the rule that 'reputations and money were made in the three-volume market' were adventure novels, children's fiction, and novels of religion, which frequently appeared in one volume (Griest 1970: 48–9).

Our data suggests that these viewpoints, while perhaps prevalent in some parts of the publishing trade, do not accurately reflect the behaviour of those producing books, those reading them, or those circulating them. Single-decker novels were the most commonly written and published, and Nesta argues that they actually sold more copies of their print runs (2007: 53). It was only in the 1880s that multivolume fiction constituted the majority of new titles (Bassett 2020: 29–30), and Mudie's stocked more single-volume novels than any other type of book. However, as Section 3.2 indicates, Mudie's took a far smaller *proportion* of what was available in one volume than it did of the available double- and triple-decker novels; presumably the principles of 'selection' were applied far more stringently to short novels than to multivolume works. Almost certainly, the prevailing viewpoint that three-volume works were 'easiest to sell' is based not on the

and would be glad to see single volumes become the standard format (Griest 1970: 173).

[57] Rhoda Broughton is described as having lost £450 by failing to expand *Second Thoughts* to three volumes (Griest 1970: 97); Nesta explores this topic in relation to George Gissing (2007: 48, 52).

aggregate numbers of novels stocked by the library but on a general perception that a single-decker novel would be judged by far more stringent standards (Griest 1970: 90). One-volume novels were relatively inexpensive, and so represented a bargain for the library – assuming, of course, that they were actually in demand from subscribers. Recalling Faux's claim that 'the best books are the best books for us', this prompts the question: how did one-volume novels fare in Mudie's, compared against multivolume works?

The casual mention of adventure novels, children's fiction and religious novels belies the importance of these genres, both in terms of their representation in the library and (at least for many examples from the first two categories) their enduring appeal to readers. As mentioned in Section 1.3.1, the 1907 catalogue provides some information on genre, which suggests that all of these types of work were present and indeed prevalent within the collection at least in 1907, with religious fiction featuring somewhat less often than the others.[58] However, the thematic index relates primarily to more recently published fiction and covers only around a third of the collection; it also offers no information on the prestige accorded to these works in their own time. One possible way in which the relative quality – or perhaps more accurately, desirability – of a novel could be measured is by its longevity within the catalogues: a work which survives longer may or may not be better than its peers, but to retain its place in the catalogue, it must have been at least

---

[58] Of the 4,886 novels in the 1907 thematic index which are listed under one or more categories, just 54 titles are described as 'Religious and Clerical', with two subcategories, 'Denomination: Controversial' and 'Roman Catholics and Proselytism'. (Books on religion are of course also listed in non-fiction.) Publishing data (see Section 3.2) suggests that Mudie's was reluctant to accept fiction from the two most prominent religious publishers, SPCK and the RTS. Meanwhile, 261 titles are listed under one or more categories which incorporate 'adventure' in its description, ranging from 'Aerial and Stellar Adventures' (16 titles) to 'West Indies/ Historical Adventures' (4 titles). The term 'adventure' in this context often denotes a fairly narrow understanding of the term – usually tales of colonial and/or martial activities – and consequently this is likely an underestimate of the number of adventure stories in the collection. While children's fiction can be harder to definitively identify, the 1907 catalogue separately lists 13 and a half double-columned pages of 'Juvenile Fiction'.

somewhat in demand. As we have seen in Section 2.4, the most common 'shelf life' of a novel in Mudie's prior to 1907 was two catalogues, and around three-quarters of titles could expect to be listed at least twice. Did novels of different lengths have measurably different shelf lives?

As it happens, for the more than 11,000 titles for which volume data is available, the average single-volume novel survived for slightly longer than its multivolume peers (see Table 10). Surprisingly, this is because a novel which was delisted after a single catalogue – indicating either a title whose appeal was short-lived, or simply a bad choice by the library – was more likely to be a multivolume work, as Table 11 indicates. Of all single-volume novels, 88.7 per cent made it into two or more catalogues, compared against 68.2 per cent of triple-deckers.

Table 10 "Shelf life" of novels in one, two, three, or additional volumes, measured by average number of catalogue appearances.

Number of vols	Average number of catalogues	Number of titles
1	2.5	5578
2	2.4	1909
3	2.2	3828
Other (4 to 36 vols)	2.7	25
All formats	2.4	11340

Table 11 Novels in one, two, or three volumes, by number of catalogue appearances.

Volumes	1 cat	2 cats	3 cats	4 cats	5 cats	6 cats	7 cats	8 cats
1	11.3%	58.7%	15.0%	8.0%	2.5%	1.6%	1.3%	1.6%
2	29.1%	35.3%	19.0%	9.6%	3.5%	1.0%	1.9%	0.5%
3	31.8%	38.1%	18.5%	7.7%	2.8%	0.6%	0.5%	0.1%

The question of whether longevity was compatible with Mudie's business model, of course, cannot be determined solely from the catalogue data – we would need to know how many copies of each work were bought, and at what price, as well as revenue from resale and subscriptions, in order to determine whether the library did better from hanging on to favourite older works or from moving them on in favour of newer ones. It may be the case that the library was more selective about which single-volume novels it purchased but was then willing to allow them a longer tenure due to their space efficiency; alternatively, their stricter selection policies may, as they claimed, have resulted in a collection with a more enduring appeal to subscribers.[59] Perhaps the one-volume novels that the library selected were, indeed, what William Faux of Smith's referred to as 'the best books' (*Publisher's Circular* 1891: 380). The library continued to stock existing triple-deckers, and list them as such, after their supposed rejection of the format: in the 1895 catalogue, a year after the ultimatum, they still represent almost 30 per cent of the collection.[60] Many of these titles – 919 in total of the three-volume novels listed in 1895 – are also to be found in the 1907 catalogue twelve years later, indicating that while new novels were no longer being published in that format, older works in three volumes held an enduring value to the library

---

[59] As mentioned previously, in some cases Mudie's appears to have replaced multi-volume novels with single-volume editions of the same text. These shrinking books, which account for around 2–6 per cent of the single-deckers in each catalogue for which we have volume data, have a much longer shelf life than most novels, being retained for 4.6 catalogues on average. The extended lifespan of these books is unsurprising given that they had achieved a second edition and that the library regarded them highly enough to purchase additional copies, and many are by well-known authors. Just 424 novels across the 20,000 listings received this treatment, and some reappear later as three-volume editions, suggesting inconsistent cataloguing; it is also possible (and indeed likely) that in some cases the library retained both editions.

[60] Bassett's (2020) suggestion that the libraries continued to purchase three-volume novels even after their ultimatum appears to be confirmed by the combined catalogues, which list many triple-deckers published in 1895 and later (although it is possible that some of these were purchased in later one-volume editions) (67).

and were still being made available to its subscribers.[61] The role of the library as a storehouse of older fiction is worth bearing in mind. Recalling William Faux's contention that the average novel spent just nine months in circulation, it is notable that Mudie's apparently held onto many of its no-longer-demanded books, either willingly (in the anticipation of the renewal of demand for an author's work due to their publishing a new novel, for example) or simply due to their being no cost-effective way to dispose of them. Either way, the catalogues demonstrate that many novels had an afterlife in Mudie's that, while perhaps offering little financial benefit to their authors, may have helped keep them relevant beyond their first flush of fame.

4.2 Defying the Libraries: Knocknagow

The beneficial effects of *inclusion* in the library's 'list' have often been asserted. In 1897, Margaret Oliphant described the impact of Mudie's public acknowledgement of a new writer's work as 'a sort of recognition from heaven' and stated that the best advertisement for a book was Mudie's announcement of 'the number of copies of it he had in circulation in his libraries' (Oliphant 1897: II, 457–8). As previously discussed, Griest's description of Mudie's as a 'guaranteed market' for fiction has been highly influential. Many novels which are now considered to be part of the nineteenth-century canon were both promoted and widely circulated by Mudie's, and some scholars have taken this as evidence that the library's strict accession policies were in fact beneficial; for example, Keith argues that 'one might generalize from [Mudie's] history that selectivity is a good thing as long as the selection is intelligently made' (1973: 372). However, the possibility remains that some of these novels might also have been successful in the absence of involvement by the major libraries. Nesta argues that the library system served only to hinder the purchase of novels by a public eager for reading material, suggesting that after 1870, increases in both the number of titles and the number of cheap editions issued by publishers are indicative of a public that was 'demanding affordable novels' (2007: 66); similarly, Bassett's quantitative analysis found that publishing

---

[61] It is possible that by 1907 some or all of this group of 919 books had been replaced with single-volume copies.

developments such as serialisation and part-publication as well as cheap reprints functioned as means by which publishers 'worked around the libraries to directly reach the reading public'. Different libraries also applied different selection policies. Keith's (surprisingly passionate) 1973 defence of Mudie reminds readers that 'his refusal to take a book did not mean that it was necessary to buy a copy abroad and smuggle it past the customs'. Amid the 1860 controversy over the library's alleged censorship of *Miriam May*, Keith points out, two of its London competitors (Bubb of New Bond Street and Hookham and Sons of Old Bond Street) had written to the *Literary Gazette* reminding readers that the novel could be borrowed from their libraries, and that it was also for sale from its publisher at a relatively affordable 10/6 (Keith 1973: 366–7).

If Mudie's declined to purchase or circulate a novel, what then? Griest argued that 'authors who ventured outside Mudie's limits were severely handicapped, and the charge of arbitrary censorship was irrefutable' (1970: 147), a conclusion with which many nineteenth-century writers were in agreement. Charles Reade, who self-published some of his own work and clashed with Mudie's on a number of occasions, described the circulating library system as 'calamitous', enabling librarians to 'hold back the good book, and substitute the trash, with dishonest excuses, in the credulous country customer's parcel' (Reade 1883: 147). A writer going by the name of 'Auctor' wrote to the *Pall Mall Gazette* in 1884 to argue that '[Mudie's] peculiar system spoils the sale of books most effectually', and details his experience of publishing 'a political biography in two volumes' which perfectly encapsulates the complaints of writers labouring within the system. This work's sales, its author believed, had been detrimentally affected by the libraries' insistence on a high initial price of 32s, as well as its early remaindering and a delayed second edition. To add insult to injury, upon requesting the book at the library, friends of the author's had been 'warned of its political tendencies' (Moore 1976: 46). Moore's aforementioned *Literature at Nurse*, while arguably serving as an advertisement for Moore's novels, also sums up a number of these critiques and puts forth an impassioned argument that Mudie's (or, more specifically, Mudie himself) was 'imped[ing] the free development of our literature' (Moore 1976: 17). Moore, who with his publisher Vizetelly had experimented with publishing works in one-volume, 6s editions, claimed that he had personally triumphed over the library's censorship through his campaigning (Griest 1970: 154). However, he was not the first writer to successfully issue a book in defiance of the library's perceived preferences. At least one example exists of a novel which enjoyed enormous sales and a lengthy literary afterlife, despite being published in a single volume at the height of the triple-decker's ascendancy, and never appearing in a Mudie's catalogue. The 1879 novel *Knocknagow; or, the Homes of Tipperary*, by Irish author Charles Kickham, was issued in a single volume by Dublin publisher James Duffy following partial serialisation. Kickham had previously been jailed for Fenian activities, and upon the serialisation of *Knocknagow* in the nationalist periodical *The Nation*, accompanied by some of his political writings, he was briefly threatened with further prosecution (Comerford 1979: 104). Mudie's views on this novel are not known, but its associations with political radicalism, and its early appearance in a single, 600-page edition priced at 3/6, suggest that it would not have been seriously considered for inclusion in the library catalogues.[62] Despite this, *Knocknagow* became a bestseller, its mix of nostalgia, tragedy and heroic action striking a chord with Irish readers that rendered it far more influential and long-lasting than his propagandist works. Considered a key source for the specific nationalist rhetoric later employed by Éamon de Valera regarding cosy homesteads, the novel retained its literary currency well into the twentieth century; it was not until the 1970s that the number of readers of Joyce's *Ulysses* is believed to have overtaken *Knocknagow* (Nolan 2007: 131, xii). Kickham's biographer estimates that following a particularly commercially successful edition of 1887, no fewer than 100,000 copies were printed in Ireland over the course of the following century (Comerford 1979: 209);[63] new editions were being published as late as the 1980s.

---

[62] James Duffy, the work's Dublin-based publisher, is not known to have had a cordial relationship with Mudie's; none of the four titles published by the firm in the ten-year sample were listed in the library's catalogues. In fact, of the six Dublin-based publishers in this sample, only William Curry had any works admitted to Mudie's.

[63] In Ireland during the 1960s, there were a sufficient number of copies still extant that both parents of the author of this Element independently read the book as children.

Bassett's analysis notes that novels appearing initially in 'inexpensive one-volume editions' were indeed published in quantity and that some were also circulated by libraries. However, he suggests that such books were often from genres such as children's fiction, sentimental tales, religious fiction, and shilling shockers, and 'generally occupied a place of lower prestige if not lower economic value in the literary marketplace' (Bassett 2020: 183). This view accords with Griest's characterisation of the one-volume novel as 'light, charming perhaps, but often questionable' in contrast to the 'substantial, accepted, conventional' three-volume novel (1970: 49). The fact that an inexpensive single-volume novel might prove resistant to the combined effects of the prestige of the triple-decker, the might of the library system, and the apparent reluctance of the public to purchase novels, in order to become 'the national epic of the Irish middle class' (Nolan 2007: xvi), does not disprove prevailing understandings about the relative status of single and multivolume novels in the nineteenth century. Rather, it demonstrates the possibilities of re-evaluating prevailing narratives about books published outside of the cultural mainstream, and their potential impacts, during the nineteenth century.

4.3 Mudie's Authors and the Royal Literary Fund

The inclusion of a novel in a Mudie's 'list', which Margaret Oliphant fondly recalled as seeming like 'recognition from heaven' in the early years of her career, has conventionally been understood as having direct financial benefits for the book's author. As Hammond argued in 2006:

> Mudie might be – and frequently was – accused of peddling worthless fiction to bored ladies and of inhibiting the progress of art, but the middle classes apparently had a strong sense of the books that it was acceptable for them to obtain through this public medium. By selling morality and conservatism, circulating libraries like Mudie's sidestepped the fiction as problem issue, made a substantial profit, and largely controlled the publishing industry for some years. **When an author was taken on by Mudie's, he or she had arrived financially.**
>
> (Hammond 2006: 28, my emphasis)

In theory, the most money was to be made with three-volume novels, whose manuscripts typically commanded higher prices from publishers. Griest asserts that 'reputations and money were made in the three-volume market' (1970: 46), and George Gissing's novelist Reardon expresses a similar viewpoint in *New Grub Street* (1891):

> An author of moderate repute may live on a yearly three-volume novel – I mean the man who is obliged to sell his book out and out, and who gets from one to two hundred pounds for it. But he would have to produce four one-volume novels to obtain the same income; and I doubt whether he could get so many published within the twelve months.
>
> (Gissing 1892: 236)

Nesta's analysis of the economics of the triple-decker, however, casts doubt upon the profitability of the format either for the publisher or its author, especially when the cost of a manuscript was over £100 (Nesta 2007: 57). An important 1990 study by S. D. Mumm, which examined applications by a number of women writers to the Royal Literary Fund, also suggests that writing was a frequently unremunerative occupation, and that while a few authors regularly received £100–£150 for their manuscripts, these were very much the minority (Mumm 1990: 7–9). Under these circumstances, did the existence of Mudie's and the library system help or hinder writers in making a living?

To answer this question, an examination was conducted of the authors with the most fictional works listed in Mudie's. There are 110 writers – not counting Anonymous – who have 30 or more novels listed in the combined catalogues. Among them we find authors who were highly popular in their lifetimes and whose works remain in print to this day, including Anthony Trollope, M. E. Braddon, James Fenimore Cooper, Wilkie Collins, Henry James, Jules Verne, Alexandre Dumas, Frances Hodgson Burnett, H. Rider Haggard, and Walter Scott. However, not all of the most prolific writers in Mudie's enjoyed this kind of enduring success. From the list of 110, 35 writers (or their surviving family members) applied to the Royal Literary Fund for financial support. In all except two of these cases, the Royal

Literary Fund provided some kind of grant, indicating that a genuine financial need had been identified.[64] Some authors applied to the fund multiple times, sometimes over numerous years, suggesting a long-term struggle for financial stability. Notable among these writers are Emma Marshall (108 novels in Mudie's, 4 applications over 7 years); Henrietta Keddie (88 novels, four applications over 19 years); Florence Warden (77 novels, ten applications over 18 years); Katharine Sarah MacQuoid (47 books, eight applications over 21 years); Joseph Smith Fletcher (35 books, seven applications over 28 years); Thomas Wilkinson Speight (34 books, four applications over 24 years); and James Edward Preston Muddock (31 books, four applications over 41 years). Tellingly, while some of these authors have received critical attention over the years, very few are mentioned by Griest. The standard history of Mudie's, while attending to many of those who struggled with or against the library, does not encompass this group who succeeded within the library and then failed anyway.

Many writers from this group of 35 were Mudie's stalwarts, producing novels which were almost guaranteed entry into library and which, once bought, were continually listed in its catalogues. For example, Henrietta Keddie ('Sarah Tytler') published her first novel in 1852 and went on to write at least ninety more: 86 of her novels are listed in the combined catalogues, and the majority of these (75) persisted in the catalogues after their first appearance. Her four applications to the Royal Literary Fund over the course of nineteen years, resulting in grants of £400 in total, suggest that the long-term retention of a novel by Mudie's was not correlated with lasting

---

[64] One case is worth mentioning here: George MacDonald's 1859 application to the Royal Literary Fund occurred quite early in his career, one year after his first novel (*Phantastes*, 1858, one volume) was published; Finkelstein's (1993) data indicates that Mudie's had taken 250 of the 1000 copies that Smith, Elder published. He subsequently published many works of poetry and fiction, including the children's novels for which he is still celebrated, and did not apply again to the Royal Literary Fund. By the 1870s, however, Sadler's entry on MacDonald in the *Dictionary of National Biography* notes that 'despite his writing and preaching without intermission, MacDonald's income was still small'. He was eventually awarded a Civil List pension of £100 per annum (Sadler 2004).

financial stability, and she was not the only such example. Walter Besant, one of the founders of the Society of Authors trade union, wrote of authorship in 1899 that 'there is life-long penury in it: starvation: suicide: a debtor's prison: hard and grinding work for miserable pay: a cruel task-master: work done to order paid for by the yard' (Besant 1899: 8). Eliot notes that Besant was a very popular writer of history and novels of social concern, whose books 'were widely circulated by Mudie's and Smith's, and which, in their cheaper versions, sold tens of thousands of copies' (Eliot 1987: 25); 46 novels which he wrote (or co-wrote with James Rice) are listed in the combined Mudie's catalogue. Despite this acclaim, Besant's widow Lady Mary Besant applied to the Royal Literary Fund for financial aid just a year after his death in 1901, and was awarded the substantial sum of £250.[65]

The range of years in which these 35 authors first applied to the Royal Literary Fund spans 1859 to 1923, with half applying for the first time after 1900; evidently, several writers from this group applied to the Royal Literary Fund toward the end of their careers, when what Besant describes as the 'hard and grinding work' of writing for a living was no longer possible. Emma Marshall was one such author; turning to novel-writing after the failure of her husband's business, she produced 'nearly 200 volumes in the evenings, after the day's labour of caring for nine children was over', over the course of twenty years, and applied to the Royal Literary Fund 'only when increasing age and debility forced her to abandon her reluctantly chosen profession' (Mumm 1990: 7). In 1887, the year in which she first applied to the Royal Literary Fund, she had published five single-volume novels (thus exceeding the upper limit suggested by Gissing in *New Grub Street*), all of which were taken by Mudie's. Even at such a rate of production, it was apparent that a comfortable retirement was by no means guaranteed. Another of the writers who appears on the list, Charlotte Riddell, would become the first pensioner of the Society of Authors; a note on her Royal Literary Fund application

---

[65] Besant's complex financial history is described by Eliot (1987): 'Despite his vigorous, even heroic campaigning for authors' rights, he often seemed almost to collude with publishers in under-selling himself. [. . .] One cannot get away from the impression that Besant sold most of his copyrights outright as soon as he could because he didn't believe that his work would last' (60).

(written by committee member J. M. Barrie) reads 'tho' once a popular writer there is now little demand for her work, and she writes so slowly nowadays that her income is almost nil. She sold all her popular books for fixed sums, and such of them as still have any sale bring her in nothing' (Kelleher 2000: 129). Fifty-one books by Riddell appear in the combined Mudie's catalogues, across six of the catalogues; almost all were continuously listed after their first acquisition. A wry comment on the publication of a new novel in *Did He Deserve It?* demonstrates Riddell's (1897) view of the role of Mudie's in the publishing industry: 'Lady Patricia, who had a frugal mind, as befitted the wife of a very rich man, felt she did her duty [to the novel] by requesting Mudie to let her have the work at once' (259). Mumm's study of women applicants to the Royal Literary Fund argues that the low price paid by publishers for copyrights was a key factor in the financial distress experienced by the writers in her study. Her work indicates that at least for the members of this group, Gissing's suggested £100 was generally out of reach, with £30 to £50 far more likely. For the women in Mumm's study, for whom the sale of copyrights was a key source of income, such low prices put them at risk of financial jeopardy.[66] The writers in Mumm's study were, by definition, struggling financially, and it would be unsurprising if they were, on average, being paid sums that were lower than the industry standard. However, it appears that a copyright price of £50 was not unusual. Nesta's analysis of the financial workings of Mudie's and the broader publishing industry argues that a novel became profitable 'only if publishers could pay little for the copyright and sell most of an edition – something that was true only if copyrights were £50 or less and sales of 40%' (Nesta 2007: 65–6). Bassett's study of publishers' records does not support this conclusion, finding that at least for Bentley, three-volume novels turned a fairly reliable profit – in part because they could reliably be sold to the circulating libraries. This work also suggests that while the other major publishing houses are generally less well attested in the surviving records, there are indications that Bentley was not unique in this regard (Bassett 2020: 142). Notably, however, while Bentley offered more

---

[66] As Mumm notes, 'Thirty-one per cent of those who reported their annual literary income earned less than £30 in that year, which was bad enough to force them to request charity' (1990: 9).

generous sums for copyrights of editions published in more than 500 copies, for small runs it was common to offer £50 or in some cases, less, for multivolume novels, especially when the author was relatively new or untried.[67]

In 1861, Wynter optimistically wrote of Mudie's that '[i]ts value to authors . . . cannot be lightly estimated, inasmuch as its machinery enables a bountiful supply of their works to be distributed to the remotest parts of the island, thereby increasing their reputation in an ever-widening circle' (Wynter 1861: 706). It may be true that the library and its distribution networks helped to introduce writers to wider audiences, yet when considered alongside the records of the Royal Literary Fund, the combined catalogues do not suggest an uncomplicated link between prominence in Mudie's and financial security. It remains unclear how those writers who produced fewer works overall (who make up the majority of the 6,000 fiction contributors to Mudie's) or whose books were rejected by the library, were financially impacted: since this cohort likely included many who wrote on a more casual basis, elucidating their experience would require extensive biographical research. Yet with around a third of the best-represented novelists in Mudie's forced to apply for charitable aid, it is clear that even those authors who seemingly should have been best able to earn a living for themselves might struggle within the library system. Mudie's themselves did not determine how much authors were paid for their work, but they played a direct role in the system that kept books expensive, publishing profits low, and manuscripts cheap. As Mumm writes, the system benefited the 'fortunate few', such as George Eliot or M. E. Braddon, who could write extensively and sell their work at a premium, yet for many writing was 'the choice of those without choices', and the library was part of the was machinery that ensured they stayed poor (Mumm 1990: 17).

[67] Publishing records for Bentley, cited in Bassett (2020), indicate that the firm purchased the copyright for at least twelve multivolume novels at £50 between 1865 and 1890. In six other cases they paid less than this, going as low as £20 for John Byrne Leicester's *A Screw Loose* in 1868. All except two of these novels made a profit for the firm (105–13, 127–9, 135–7). Bassett notes that if a book was successful, its author would generally earn more for subsequent works.

4.4 Male and Female Authorship in Mudie's

Some scholarship on women's authorship of English-language fiction in the nineteenth century has argued for a general decline in the overall proportion of titles published by women, which began in the early 1800s. The *Waverley* novels are often seen as a key instigating incident in what Garside has described as a 'general masculinization of the novel both in terms of authorship and readers' (2013: 22). Not only were Walter Scott's historical novels accorded more prestige than had been previously the case for long-form prose fiction but, following the publication of *Kenilworth* in a three-volume, 31s 6d edition, they were also instrumental in setting the standard format and price for the 'prestige' three-decker novel for almost the rest of the century. An influential sociological work in this area, Tuchman's (2012) *Edging Women Out*, argues that the history of the English novel illustrates the 'empty field phenomenon', in which as a previously low-status occupation grows more prestigious, it is increasingly occupied by men. In an analysis of the contents of the HathiTrust digital collection, Underwood (2019) concurs with Tuchman, finding that from the middle of the nineteenth century onward, a decline occurred in the percentage of English-language fiction titles written by women that would not be reversed until the 1970s (158). However, more recent bibliographical scholarship has called some of these arguments into question due to concerns over the datasets and methodologies they employ.[68] Conflicting with the concept of women being 'edged out', Bassett's 2020 study found that, at least in respect to multivolume fiction, women's contribution was robust and ongoing, outpacing that of men at some points during the nineteenth century, and that 'women authors were primarily responsible for the surge in multivolume fiction production in the late 1870s and early 1880s' (49).

How can Mudie's library catalogues contribute to this discussion? The interests of the library did not always coincide with those of the wider publishing industry, and its fiction collection did not directly reflect the body of available published fiction, given that they (at least nominally)

---

[68] Riddell and Bassett (2021) note significant issues with the HathiTrust's metadata; Weedon (2019) registers concern with the sampling methods employed by Tuchman (39–40).

retained and emphasised the right to choose which works to purchase. The question of whether Mudie's reflected or departed from gender trends in the broader publishing industry, therefore, is worth considering, particularly in light of the library's scale and degree of influence.

A comparable previous study of nineteenth-century library catalogues found that that novels by women were numerically and proportionally underrepresented in colonial libraries across the southern hemisphere, despite women publishing more titles overall (Wade and Fermanis 2023: 95). While proportions varied across times and places, the smaller libraries in this set typically stocked fewer works by women and vice versa, reflecting the tendency toward excessive 'canonicity' – and hence, maleness – which Franco Moretti observed in relation to small libraries (Moretti 1997: 154). If this logic were to hold true for Mudie's, one of the largest libraries then in existence globally, it would suggest that the library should hold women's fiction in proportions close to what was being published – or at least, that it should be less male-dominated than the small, geographically dispersed libraries considered by Wade and Fermanis. An examination of the combined Mudie's catalogues, as shown in Table 12, indicates that women were indeed better represented in Mudie's than in smaller contemporary institutions. While percentages fluctuate from catalogue to catalogue, throughout the whole period under consideration, women's writings did constitute a significant proportion of the library's fiction collection, and sometimes represented a majority.

Across the eighty-year period, for books attributed to a single author, 42.8 per cent were written by women, with 52.8 per cent attributed to men. Another 4.5 per cent are from writers whose identity is uncertain and are designated 'Other'.[69] (Books attributed to two or more authors account for just 322 of the novels in the collection, about 1.5 per cent.[70])

---

[69] The gender categories used in this study are female, male, and other, which includes works of unknown, anonymous, pseudonymous, and multiple authorship. While an extremely simplified scheme of gender representation, it allows for an understanding of the degree to which members of the different categories were represented.

[70] Of the 322 multiply-authored novels, most (145) are attributed to two men; 91 were co-written by a man and a woman, and 38 by two women. The remainder are attributed to a variety of different multi-author teams.

Table 12 Gender breakdown of books in Mudie's catalogues written by individual authors.

Number of titles

	1848–9	1857	1860	1865	1876	1885	1895	1907	All catalogues
Female	251	502	608	923	1651	2520	3916	5891	9035
Male	484	637	685	997	1515	1965	3896	8649	11143
Other	11	39	59	109	200	205	316	482	940
All	746	1178	1352	2029	3366	4690	8128	15022	21118

Percentage of titles

	1848–9	1857	1860	1865	1876	1885	1895	1907	All catalogues
Female	33.6%	42.6%	45.0%	45.5%	49.0%	53.7%	48.2%	39.2%	42.8%
Male	64.9%	54.1%	50.7%	49.1%	45.0%	41.9%	47.9%	57.6%	52.8%
Other	1.5%	3.3%	4.4%	5.4%	5.9%	4.4%	3.9%	3.2%	4.5%

How did these proportions vary over time? Examining the discrete catalogues, we see a gradual increase in female authorship, from a low of 33.6 per cent in the first catalogue, to a late-century peak of three catalogues in which women's fiction overtakes that of men – 1876, 1885, and 1895 – before dropping back somewhat, to below 40 per cent, in 1907.[71] This peak in the 1880s coincides with what Bassett has identified as a 'surge in multi-volume fiction production in the late 1870s and early 1880s' which was propelled by women authors (2020: 49), suggesting that Mudie's either followed the trail being set by publishers, or contributed to the popularity of long-form women's fiction by purchasing and circulating it widely – or perhaps both.

However, since Mudie's retained older works as well as buying in new fiction, catalogue breakdowns do not necessarily correspond to its buying policies year-on-year. In order to gain an understanding of which texts were being purchased by the library, and by which authors, on an ongoing basis, some comparisons with ATCL data from the ten-year sample set are helpful.

If we look at multivolume novels in the library, it is clear that Mudie's purchased the vast majority of what was available, which is unsurprising given the findings described in Section 3.2. Women's multivolume fiction, overall, was slightly more likely to be accepted for the library's collection than that of men; as was also the case for the libraries surveyed in Wade and Fermanis, fiction in the 'other' category was the least likely to have been acquired, suggesting that libraries and their readers valued identifiable authorship (see Table 13).

While these overall figures indicate that Mudie's took just under 80 per cent of all multivolume novels from the sample years, if we break them down on a year-by-year basis, it becomes clear that, as previously demonstrated, a change in selection policy took place after 1852, and the

---

[71] It is unclear why the 1907 catalogue demonstrates this shift toward male authors, but 61 per cent of its fiction collection had been recently acquired, and this cohort was more likely to be male-authored. Just under 60 per cent of the works which appear in the 1907 catalogue for the first time are male-authored, with 37 per cent written by women; of the 38.5 per cent of the collection which had appeared at least once previously, 54 per cent was by men and 43 per cent by women.

Table 13 Percentage of multivolume titles in the ten-year sample which were acquired by Mudie's, by author gender.

	Rejected	Accepted	All		%Rejected	%Accepted
Female	87	439	526	Female	16.5%	83.5%
Male	90	355	445	Male	20.2%	79.8%
Other	36	39	75	Other	48.0%	52.0%
Total	213	833	1046	Total	20.4%	79.6%

library rejected very few multivolume novels from 1855 onward (see Table 14). While fiction in the 'other' authorship category was sometimes at a disadvantage, multivolume novels by both men and women were highly acceptable from 1855 onward, with women's even more so than men's: in 1874, Mudie's took seventy-two of the seventy-three multivolume novels published by women.

However, multivolume fiction represents only part of the picture; as we have seen, Mudie's collection was often dominated by single-volume novels, and women produced shorter fiction in significant quantities. How did single-deckers by men and women fare in the library's collection?

Complete comparative data from 1880 onward is not available for single-volume novels, which is unfortunate due to their increasing importance as the century continued. However, as shown in Table 15, the data up to the 1870s indicates that while Mudie's acquired fewer single-volume novels for their collection across the board. women's single-volume fiction was generally as acceptable to the library as men's, and sometimes more so.

As well as being one of the key buyers of novels published in any given year, Mudie's also preserved and provided long-term access to older novels that still held some interest to readers. As Section 4.3 discusses, this may have worked against the financial interests of individual owners and publishers, by providing the public with a stockpile of borrowable novels which mitigated against calls for further editions. However, it did have the result of keeping older works visible in the form of the 'lists', and also aided in the circulation of titles throughout the world by supplying books to

Table 14 Multivolume titles in the ten-year sample, by year.

	All titles published in 2, 3, and 4 vols				All titles in Mudie's in 2, 3, and 4 vols				% in Mudie's in 2, 3, and 4 vols			
	Female	Male	Other	All	Female	Male	Other	All	Female	Male	Other	All
1842	27	33	5	65	5	11		16	18.5%	33.3%	0.0%	24.6%
1845	31	41	9	81	13	24	2	39	41.9%	58.5%	22.2%	48.1%
1852	44	30	7	81	20	13		33	45.5%	43.3%	0.0%	40.7%
1855	28	25	10	63	26	22	9	57	92.9%	88.0%	90.0%	90.5%
1858	54	25	2	81	51	21	2	74	94.4%	84.0%	100.0%	91.4%
1863	52	63	8	123	48	56	8	104	92.3%	88.9%	100.0%	84.6%
1874	73	72	13	158	72	62	9	143	98.6%	86.1%	69.2%	90.5%
1883	126	68	15	209	115	62	12	189	91.3%	91.2%	80.0%	90.4%
1893	91	88	6	185	89	84	5	178	97.8%	95.5%	83.3%	96.2%
1899	0	0	0	0	0	0	0	0				
All	526	445	75	1046	439	355	47	833	83.5%	79.8%	62.7%	79.6%

Table 15 Single-volume titles in the ten-year sample, by year.

	All titles, single volume				All titles in Mudie's, single volume				% titles in Mudie's, single volume			
	Female	Male	Other	All	Female	Male	Other	All	Female	Male	Other	All
1842	10	15	1	26	3	3		6	30.0%	20.0%	0.0%	23.1%
1845	13	21	1	35	2	10	1	13	15.4%	47.6%	100.0%	37.1%
1852	31	36	10	77	10	18	1	29	32.3%	50.0%	10.0%	37.7%
1855	42	43	5	91	16	13		29	38.1%	30.2%	0.0%	31.9%
1858	49	48	14	111	22	22	1	45	44.9%	45.8%	7.1%	40.5%
1863	88	80	57	225	31	22	6	53	35.2%	27.5%	10.5%	23.6%
1874	154	94	45	293	50	26	6	82	32.5%	27.7%	13.3%	28.0%
All	387	337	133	858	134	114	15	257	34.6%	33.8%	11.3%	30.0%

smaller libraries and other subsidiaries (Roberts 2006: 15). Women's fiction, as Table 16 shows, was on average retained slightly longer in Mudie's catalogues than that of men.

In relation to longevity, Fryckstedt's reading of Mudie's as serving a number of different intergenerational needs is thought-provoking enough to deserve quoting in full:

> Although there was a significant shift of taste in the 1860s when most readers were drawn away from the tame precincts of the domestic novel to spicier regions, there were still readers, judging from Mudie's catalogues, who continued to read domestic love stories to the end of the Victorian period. It is in fact remarkable that they did survive in such numbers. They did so because they reminded readers of what in retrospect seemed a more stable society in which men and women had their given roles. Perhaps novels like *Rachel Gray* and *Clarinda Singlehart* were also bought or borrowed by parents who, themselves preferring Ouida's and Rhoda Broughton's 'wicked' novels for literary entertainment, wanted their offspring to imbibe the values that had prevailed in their own youth, values to which they subscribed at least sentimentally, although it became harder to believe in their validity in a world that was changing beyond recognition.
>
> (Fryckstedt 1987: 22)

Table 16 Shelf life of a novel in Mudie's (average catalogue count), by author gender.

Author gender	Number of titles	Average catalogue count per title
Female	9140	1.79
Male	11346	1.69
Other	1546	1.48
Total	22032	

This provides a compelling explanation for the longevity of works by writers in the domestic genre, but notably, the 'wicked' novels of Broughton, Ouida, and sensation novelists such as M. E. Braddon and Mrs Henry Wood were also bought and held in the library almost without interruption. As Section 4.3 has argued, this did not necessarily mean that the authors of these works were making a steady living; Marie Louise de la Ramée, who wrote as 'Ouida', received a grant of £300 from the Royal Literary Fund, and a majority of the applicants to the Royal Literary Fund described in Section 4.3 were female.[72] However, it does demonstrate that fiction of multiple kinds, and from multiple genres, could coexist for long periods of time within this most capacious of libraries, perhaps precisely because it could simultaneously cater to the preferences of the Victorians of different generations who might share a household and a subscription.

The respectability and improving quality of all works in Mudie's library was, of course, a key selling point for the library. Non-fiction was emphasised (sometimes above fiction); Fryckstedt notes the prominence given in advertisements to 'works of history, biography, religion, philosophy and travel', with fiction relegated to a secondary position (Fryckstedt 1987: 10). Griest, describing what she calls the 'young girl standard', argues that a library catering to the Victorian public inevitably had to impress upon their subscription base that all of their novels were appropriate for a family audience, especially in a time where reading aloud was common, and that this was precisely what Mudie had achieved (1970: 137).

> No longer would the head of a Victorian family need to waste his time scanning circulating library works to see whether they were suitable for his daughters; no longer would the daughter, like Lydia Languish, have to throw her book behind the sofa at the entrance of her parent; the Mudie

[72] The 35 Royal Literary Fund applications were made on behalf of sixteen female and nineteen male writers. However, if we take into account that applications were often made by writers' surviving family members, the gender split is in fact twenty-six female applicants, eight male, and one made first by novelist James Grant and subsequently by his widow.

> novel, resplendent in its bright yellow cover imprinted with
> the Pegasus symbol, lay on the parlor table, ready for any
> member of the family circle to read aloud.
>
> (Griest 1970: 18)

Roberts has argued that while the appearance of a book in the catalogue implied that it had already been preselected for quality and appropriateness, 'the sense of exclusiveness which Mudie's fostered was based more on his rhetoric of selection than on the actual novels selected' (2006: 13). Our data supports these conclusions. Selection was applied unevenly at best, and the library was in many ways comparable, in terms of what it held, with the earlier libraries that were renowned for conveying 'trash' to the public. The 'young girl' standard was equally illusory, as the quote from *Miss Blanchard of Chicago*, at the opening of this Element, makes clear. Miss Vie Carlisle is an avid consumer of alarmingly forward-thinking non-fiction (essays on socialism, histories of heathen religions, 'theosophic works'), but as someone who enjoys a good society novel, she is also well supplied by her Mudie's subscription. Other characters from nineteenth-century novels recall the opening of the 'Mudie box' as an almost illicit pleasure, as is described in Mrs Randolph's *Genista*:

> [Diana] preferred coiling herself up behind one of the large sofas
> in the saloon so as to be invisible even to Aunt Prissy's searching
> eyes if she entered the room, and devouring the novels out of
> Mudie's box, which, though they had never been positively
> prohibited, would certainly have been so had the idea of the
> children touching them ever occurred to Miss Priscilla's mind.
>
> (Randolph 1879: I, 37).

In reality, as Colclough's work on sensation fiction also demonstrates, if given unrestricted access to the Mudie's catalogue, the resourceful young woman reader could certainly find materials that might otherwise be denied entry to the Victorian household by the traditional paterfamilias.

Despite the evident ineffectiveness of attempts at protecting young women from their own reading preferences, the library's 'selection' has often been portrayed in highly gendered terms. In 1894, George Moore described the 'strength, *virility*, and purpose' (my emphasis) of British literature as being threatened by 'the commercial views of a narrow-minded tradesman', with the feminising effects of the library further emphasised by his assertion that 'literature is now rocked to an ignoble rest in the motherly arms of the librarian' (Moore 1976: 18).[73] Pierre Coustillas, Moore's twentieth-century editor, enthusiastically endorsed Moore's criticisms, claiming that 'as three-volume fiction found a notable portion of its readers among the idle females of the middle-classes whose view of life was narrow, the artist's freedom in the choice and treatment of his subject thus was severely restricted' (Moore 1976: 13). As late as 2006, one scholar would casually note that 'Mudie might be – and frequently was – accused of peddling worthless fiction to bored ladies and of inhibiting the progress of art' (Hammond 2006: 28). Such commentary fails to take into account the complexity of the relationships between the library's female readers and writers. Female figures such as the young, innocent reader and the formidable 'matron' who protected her were invoked to justify the library's existence, as a mechanism for funnelling suitable literature to the heart of the Victorian family. Meanwhile, the real women who were blamed for 'inhibiting the progress of art' by relying on the circulating libraries for their reading materials were also some of its most prolific, and apparently valued, contributors, who themselves broke the boundaries of propriety and conventionalism on occasion.

---

[73] Moore's comments should be understood as part of a long-running public campaign against what he perceived as the censorship of his work, in which Mudie – both librarian and library – provided a convenient antagonist, despite being just one player within the library system (see Bassett 2005). His enthusiasm was no doubt at least partly based on a genuine sense of injustice, but it also (as Keith points out) served as a form of advertising for his novels (Keith 1973: 371).

5 Conclusion

[T]he larger our libraries are the greater the impossibility of knowing what they consist of.

'Hints on Reading' (*The Lady's Magazine* 1789: 79)

In 1894, an article on Mudie's in *Good Words* concluded sombrely of the many 'books of the once-idolised author' which were now consigned to storage in Mudie's cellars, that 'here [they] must lie, immured in these catacombs, unless some grand cremation should reduce them to ashes' (Preston 1894: 671). Just under twenty years later, in June 1913, such an event did in fact occur at the New Oxford Street branch of Mudie's. Perhaps a fire was inevitable given the extent of the flammable materials held on the premises; in 1865 a smaller fire at their Manchester branch had caused an estimated £5,000 of damage (*East London Advertiser* 1865). This time, the conflagration – apparently originating in one of the library's store-rooms – quickly took 'so firm a hold that the back portion of the premises were burnt out and the flames burst through the roof'; the fire took several hours to extinguish, and caused a gas explosion which collapsed a staircase and caused 'narrow escapes' for several firemen. While the fire was eventually contained, at least 30,000 books were destroyed, many apparently 'of considerable value owing to their rarity and age': the *Times* reported that 'it is unlikely that more than a few of them can be replaced' (*Times* 1913: 10). In undergoing the 'grand cremation' foreseen by Preston in 1894, the 'dead stock ... immured' in Mudie's 'catacombs' had been transmuted into irreplaceable and valued literary heritage. As this work has sought to demonstrate, the discourses surrounding the circulating library – its seemingly incalculably vast collection and equally limitless power – have often been contradictory, informed by the multiplicity of different and often competing viewpoints of those who participated in the literary and publishing cultures of Victorian Britain. In the absence of complete records of the library's day-to-day functioning, even the most thorough and deeply considered accounts of a complex and long-lived institution may be led into inaccurate views of events. Griest wryly gestures towards this difficulty in describing an 1884 newspaper debate following criticisms of the library by George Moore, in which 'every viewpoint from wholehearted approval of the library system to complete endorsement of Moore's opinions [were] represented with, as usual, anecdotes of personal experiences to support claims on both sides' (Griest 1970: 83–4). Katz, in describing the same set of discussions surrounding the library, notes that 'to write about this debate is to engage with a key historiographical problem: the imposition of order on a disparate community engaged in discrete conversations' (2017: 406). In creating the combined catalogues, this work has sought not to supplant previous understandings of Mudie's library but to augment them, in accordance with a practice that Katharine Bode has termed 'data-rich literary history'. Bode has argued for the need for 'scholarly editions of literary systems', which may take the form of 'a curated dataset' modelling 'the editor's argument about the nature of and relationships between literary works in the past'. In examining quantitative data from the combined catalogues in conversation with other sources of information on the library, ranging from massive datasets such as Bassett's *At The Circulating Library* to individual letters from Mudie's correspondence, this Element represents an attempt to create what Bode calls a critical apparatus, explaining

> the history of transmission that the editor's understanding is based upon and contributes to, while the curated text embodies the outcome of that history of transmission, including the current moment of interpretation, in the form of a stable, historicized, and publicly accessible object for analysis.
>
> (Bode 2018: 7)

The representation of Mudie's collection is a flat one – we may know which works the library chose to advertise to its customers, but the number of copies taken, and the exact system of readers and reviewers they employed, remains generally unknown to us, and the catalogues can only allow us to guess at these. As has been emphasised, the combined catalogue is incomplete, both due to the intentions and purposes of their original designers, and because of the scope and focus of this project. Yet, the catalogues remain a valuable source of information not only on the public availability of the books they contain and those who produced them, but also in themselves, as 'organizational sites that encode raced and gendered categories of knowledge' and 'construct hierarchies of commercial and literary value' (Wade and Fermanis 2023: 72). Bode reminds us that 'pre-digital traditions, ideologies, and infrastructures also shape digital resources and methods in substantial and influential ways'. In an era in which mass-digitised heritage collections have become both increasingly common and increasingly serve as the basis for scholarly work, work such as Riddell and Bassett's 2021 study of the HathiTrust collection of novels from 1836 and 1838 illustrates the need for detailed consideration of the histories of our historical collections. As Riddell and Bassett found in this collection, multi-volume novels by men were most likely to have been digitised at least once, with single-volume novels, novels by women, and novels by authors of unknown gender less likely to have been digitised. Such findings are remarkably similar to the understandings of literary prestige which have been described and challenged in this work, and indicate that the circumstances in which historical materials were created continue to have an impact on how those materials are preserved, used, and understood.

The construction of the combined Mudie's catalogues represents an effort to bridge the mass-digitised collection and the more intimate, individual scale of close reading by providing critical context about the ways in which works emerged into and – in most cases – eventually dropped out of the view of the public. What this allows us is another view on a key time period in the development of the English novel, during which the size of the reading public, and its demand for reading matter, underwent an enormous expansion alongside social and technological changes which made printed materials cheaper and more broadly available. In providing a new history of novels in Mudie's library, this Element proposes also that the combined catalogues, in representing what Keith terms 'an index of popularity' (1973: 372), may serve as a kind of filter or baseline for mass-digitised collections of texts, pinpointing a selection of titles which were available to (and perhaps cherished by) a given portion of the reading public in a particular time, yet which must always be considered in light of the specific contexts governing the acquisition, maintenance, and eventual death of items in the collection.

References

Ahnert, Ruth, Emma Griffin, Mia Ridge, and Giorgia Tolfo. 'Collaborative Historical Research in the Age of Big Data: Lessons from an Interdisciplinary Project'. *Elements in Historical Theory and Practice*, Jan. 2023. https://doi.org/10.1017/9781009175548.

Allen, Walter Ernest. *The English Novel: A Short Critical History*. Dutton, 1955.

Altick, Richard Daniel. *The English Common Reader: A Social History of the Mass Reading Public, 1800–1900*. University of Chicago Press, 1957.

Anesko, Michael. *'Friction with the Market': Henry James and the Profession of Authorship*. Oxford University Press, 1986.

Atkin, Lara, Sarah Comyn, Porscha Fermanis, and Nathan Garvey. *Early Public Libraries and Colonial Citizenship in the British Southern Hemisphere*. Springer International, 2019.

Bassett, Troy J. 'Circulating Morals: George Moore's Attack on Late-Victorian Literary Censorship'. *Pacific Coast Philology*, vol. 40, no. 2, 2005, pp. 73–89.

Bassett, Troy J. *The Rise and Fall of the Victorian Three-Volume Novel*. Springer International, 2020. *ProQuest Ebook Central*, http://ebookcentral.proquest.com/lib/ucd/detail.action?docID=6109019.

Bassett, Troy J. 2017. 'Evidence of Reading: The Social Network of the Heath Book Club'. *Victorian Studies*, vol. 59, no. 3, pp. 426–35.

Bassett, Troy J. 'Analysis: General Statistics'. *At the Circulating Library: A Database of Victorian Fiction, 1837–1901*, 2024a, www.victorianresearch.org/atcl/statistics.php.

Bassett, Troy J. *At the Circulating Library: A Database of Victorian Fiction, 1837–1901*, 2024b, www.victorianresearch.org/atcl/index.php.

Bassett, Troy J. 'Documentation'. *At the Circulating Library: A Database of Victorian Fiction, 1837–1901*, 2024c, www.victorianresearch.org/atcl/documentation.php.

Besant, Walter. *The Pen and the Book*. Thomas Burleigh, 1899.

Blakey, Dorothy. *The Minerva Press, 1790–1820*. Printed for the Bibliographical Society at the University Press, Oxford, 1939.

Bode, Katherine. *A World of Fiction: Digital Collections and the Future of Literary History*. University of Michigan Press, 2018.

Britton, John. *The Original Picture of London*. Longman, 1826.

Colclough, Stephen. 'Miss Cathy's Riven Th' Back off "Th' Helmet Uh Salvation"': Representing Book Destruction in Mid-Victorian Print Culture'. *Book Destruction from the Medieval to the Contemporary*, edited by Gill Partington and Adam Smyth. Springer, 2014, pp. 135–51.

Colclough, Stephen. 'New Innovations in Audience Control: The Select Library and Sensation'. *Reading and the Victorians*, edited by Judith John. Routledge, 2016, pp. 31–45.

Comerford, Richard Vincent. *Charles J. Kickham: A Study in Irish Nationalism and Literature*. Wolfhound Press, 1979.

Davies, Albert Kevill. *Miss Blanchard of Chicago*. F. V. White & Co, 1892.

Dike, Edwin Berck. 'Coleridge Marginalia in Henry Brooke's "The Fool of Quality"'. *The Huntington Library Bulletin*, no. 2, 1931, pp. 149–63.

Dolin, Tim. 'First Steps toward a History of the Mid-Victorian Novel in Colonial Australia'. *Australian Literary Studies*, vol. 22, no. 3, Apr. 2006, pp. 273–293.

Dwor, Richa. 'Grace Aguilar's Defence of Jewish Difference: Representing Women's Reading'. *Literature and Theology*, vol. 29, no. 1, 2015, pp. 86–103.

East London Advertiser. 'Destructive Fire at Mudie's Library, Manchester'. *East London Advertiser*, 398th ed., 30 Dec. 1865, p. 2.

Ebbes, Verena, Peter Garside, Angela Koch, Anthony Mandal, and Rainer Schöwerling. *The English Novel, 1830–1836: A Bibliographical Survey of Fiction Published in the British Isles*. 21 Nov. 2016, www.romtext.org.uk/resources/english-novel-1830-36/.

Edwards, Amelia. Letter from Amelia B. Edwards to Charles E. Mudie, November 22, 1865. https://digital.library.illinois.edu/items/856d6980-02dd-013a-7ab5-02d0d7bfd6e4-0.

Eliot, Simon. 'The Three-Decker Novel and Its First Cheap Reprint, 1862–94'. *The Library*, vol. s6-VII, no. 1, Mar. 1985, pp. 38–53.

Eliot, Simon. '"His Generation Read His Stories". Walter Besant, Chatto and Windus and "All Sorts and Conditions of Men"'. *Publishing History*, vol. 21, 1987, p. 25.

Eliot, Simon. 'Fiction and Non-Fiction: One- and Three-Volume Novels in Some Mudie Catalogues, 1857–94'. *Publishing History*, vol. 66, 2009, pp. 31–47.

Espinasse, Francis. *Literary Recollections and Sketches*. Hodder and Stoughton, 1893.

Fergus, Jan. 'Eighteenth-Century Readers in Provincial England: The Customers of Samuel Clay's Circulating Library and Bookshop in Warwick, 1770–72'. *The Papers of the Bibliographical Society of America*, vol. 78, no. 2, 1984, pp. 155–213.

Finkelstein, David. '"The Secret": British Publishers and Mudie's Struggle for Economic Survival 1861–64'. *Publishing History*, vol. 34, 1993, p. 21.

Fothergill, Caroline. *The Comedy of Cecilia: Or, An Honourable Man*. A. and C. Black, 1895.

Freeman's Journal. 'Fire at Mudie's Library'. *Freeman's Journal and Daily Commercial Advertiser*, 7 June 1913.

Fryckstedt, Monica Correa. 'Defining the Domestic Genre: English Women Novelists of the 1850s'. *Tulsa Studies in Women's Literature*, vol. 6, no. 1, 1987, pp. 9–25.

Fryckstedt, Monica Correa. 'Food for Thought: Mudie's Select Library and the Fiction of the 1860s'. *Australasian Journal of Victorian Studies*, vol. 1, no. 1, 1995, pp. 23–30.

Garside, Peter. 'The Early 19th-Century English Novel, 1820–1836'. *The Oxford Handbook of the Victorian Novel*, edited by Lisa Rodensky. Oxford University Press, 2013, pp. 21–40.

Garside, Peter, Jacqueline Belanger, and Sharon Ragaz. *British Fiction 1800–1829*. 2004, www.british-fiction.cf.ac.uk/index.html.

Gerrard, Teresa, and Alexis Weedon. 'The "Lower Classes Are Very Hard Readers": Kidderminster Municipal Library 1855–1856'. *Library & Information History*, vol. 29, May 2013, pp. 81–102. ResearchGate, https://doi.org/10.1179/1758348913Z.00000000031.

Gerrard, Teresa, and Alexis Weedon. 'Working-Class Women's Education in Huddersfield: A Case Study of the Female Educational Institute Library, 1856–1857'. *Information & Culture*, vol. 49, no. 2, Mar. 2014, pp. 234–65. https://doi.org/10.7560/IC49205.

Gipps (Mrs. Pemberton), Helen Etough. *The World's Furniture*. Skeet, 1861.

Gissing, George. *New Grub Street*. Smith, Elder, 1892.

Gladstone, William Ewart. 'Paper Duty – Adjourned Debate. (Hansard, 12 May 1852)'. *Hansard*, 12 May 1852, https://api.parliament.uk/historic-hansard/commons/1852/may/12/paper-duty-adjourned-debate.

Gohdes, Clarence. 'British Interest in American Literature during the Latter Part of the Nineteenth Century as Reflected by Mudie's Select Library'. *American Literature*, vol. 13, no. 4, 1942, pp. 356–62.

Griest, Guinevere L. *Mudie's Circulating Library and the Victorian Novel*. David & Charles, 1970.

Hammond, Mary. *Reading, Publishing and the Formation of Literary Taste in England, 1880–1914*. Ashgate, 2006.

Hardcastle, Charlotte. *A Troubled Stream*. T. C. Newby, 1866.

Herrnstein Smith, Barbara. 'What Was "Close Reading"? A Century of Method in Literary Studies'. *Minnesota Review*, vol. 87, no. 1, 2016, pp. 57–75.

Hiley, Nicholas. '"Can't You Find Me Something Nasty?" Circulating Libraries and Literary Censorship in Britain from the 1890s to the 1910s'. *Censorship and the Control of Print in England and France, 1600–1910*, edited by Robin Myers and Michael Harris. St Paul's Bibliographies, 1992, pp. 123–47.

Howell, Jordan. 'Eighteenth-Century Abridgements of Robinson Crusoe'. *The Library*, vol. 15, no. 3, Sept. 2014, pp. 292–343.

Hudson, Hannah Doherty. *Romantic Fiction and Literary Excess in the Minerva Press Era*. Cambridge University Press, 2023.

Jacobs, Edward. 'Circulating Libraries'. *The Oxford Encyclopedia of British Literature*, edited by David Scott Kastan. Oxford University Press, 2006. www.oxfordreference.com/view/10.1093/acref/9780195169218.001.0001/acref-9780195169218-e-0102.

Joshi, Priya. *In Another Country: Colonialism, Culture, and the English Novel in India*. Columbia University Press, 2002.

Katz, Peter J. 'Redefining the Republic of Letters: The Literary Public and Mudie's Circulating Library'. *Journal of Victorian Culture*, vol. 22, no. 3, Sept. 2017, pp. 399–417.

Kaufman, Paul. *Borrowings from the Bristol Library, 1773–1784: A Unique Record of Reading Vogues*. Bibliographical Society of the University of Virginia, 1960.

Kaufman, Paul. 'The Community Library: A Chapter in English Social History'. *Transactions of the American Philosophical Society*, vol. 57, no. 7, 1967, pp. 1–67.

Keith, Sara. *Mudie's Select Library: Sara Keith Collection*. c. 1955–c. 1972, https://archives.libraries.london.ac.uk/Details/archive/110035865.

http://www.senatehouselibrary.ac.uk/our-collections/historic-collections/archives-manuscripts/, 1955.

Keith, Sara. 'Literary Censorship and Mudie's Library'. *Colorado Quarterly*, vol. 21, no. 3, Winter 1973, pp. 359–72.

Kelleher, Margaret. 'Charlotte Riddell's A Struggle for Fame: The Field of Women's Literary Production'. *Colby Quarterly*, vol. 36, no. 2, Jan. 2000, pp. 116–31.

Lady's Magazine. The Lady's Magazine; Or, Entertaining Companion for the Fair Sex, Appropriated Solely to Their Use and Amusement . . . G. Robinson, 1789.

Leary, Patrick. 'Fraser's Magazine' and the Literary Life, 1830–1847'. *Victorian Periodicals Review*, vol. 27, no. 2, 1994, pp. 105–26.

Leavy, Susan, Gerardine Meaney, Karen Wade, and Derek Greene. 'Curatr: A Platform for Semantic Analysis and Curation of Historical Literary Texts'. *Metadata and Semantic Research*, edited by Emmanouel Garoufallou Francesca Fallucchi, and Ernesto William De Luca. Springer International Publishing, 2019, pp. 354–66. Springer Link, https://doi.org/10.1007/978-3-030-36599-8_31.

Lindsay, Jack. *George Meredith*. The Bodley Head, 1956.

London Society. 'Going to Mudie's'. *London Society: A Monthly Magazine of Light and Amusing Literature for the Hours of Relaxation*, vol. 16, no. 95, Nov. 1869.

Lounger at the Clubs. 'The Literary Lounger: Under the Ban and Father Sterling'. *Illustrated Times*, 22 Oct. 1864, p. 7.

Manning, Anne. Letter from Anne Manning to Charles E. Mudie, 19 Apr. 1866, https://digital.library.illinois.edu/items/85f98840-02dd-013a-7ab5-02d0d7bfd6e4-3. Illinois Library Digital Collections.

Manning, Anne. Letter from Anne Manning to Charles E. Mudie, 11 May 1866, https://digital.library.illinois.edu/items/85fcb0a0-02dd-013a-7ab5-02d0d7bfd6e4-5. Illinois Library Digital Collections.

Maturin, Charles Robert. 'Art. II – Harrington and Ormond, Tales'. *The British Review and London Critical Journal*, vol. 11, 1818, pp. 37–61.

McGrigor Allan, James. *Loan 96 RLF 1/1689/2 James McGrigor Allan to Octavian Blewitt*. 1 Jan. 1866. British Library Western Manuscripts Collection.

McGrigor Allan, James. *Loan 96 RLF 1/1689/8 Printed Letter from James McGrigor Allan to Charles Edward Mudie on the Audience for Novels*. 2 Aug. 1864. British Library Western Manuscripts Collection.

McKitterick, David. 'Second-Hand and Old Books'. *The Cambridge History of the Book in Britain: Volume 6, 1830–1914*, edited by David McKitterick. Cambridge University Press, 2009, pp. 635–73.

McNee, Alan. *The Cockney Who Sold the Alps: Albert Smith and the Ascent of Mont Blanc*. Victorian Secrets Limited, 2015.

Moore, George. *Literature at Nurse: Or, Circulating Morals: A Polemic on Victorian Censorship*, edited by Pierre Coustillas, The Harvester Press, 1976.

Moretti, Franco. 'Narrative Markets, ca. 1850'. *Review (Fernand Braudel Center)*, vol. 20, no. 2, 1997, pp. 151–74.

Mudie, Charles Edward. 'Mr. Mudie's Library'. *The Athenaeum*, 6 Oct. 1860, p. 451.

Mudie's Select Library. 'Amusement for Long Voyages'. *Mudie's Library Circular*, s.n., 1862.

Mumm, Susan D. 'Writing for Their Lives: Women Applicants to The Royal Literary Fund'. *Publishing History*, no. 27, 1990, pp. 27–49.

Nesta, Frederick. 'The Myth of the "Triple-Headed Monster": The Economics of the Three-Volume Novel'. *Publishing History*, vol. 61, 2007, pp. 47–69.

Nolan, Emer. *Catholic Emancipations: Irish Fiction from Thomas Moore to James Joyce*. Syracuse University Press, 2007.

Oliphant, Mrs (Margaret). *Annals of a Publishing House: William Blackwood and His Sons, Their Magazine and Friends*. C. Scribner's Sons, 1897.

Oliphant, Mrs (Margaret), et al. *Women Novelists of Queen Victoria's Reign: A Book of Appreciations*. Hurst & Blackett, 1897.

Palgrave, Francis Turner. Letter from Francis Palgrave to Charles E. Mudie, 8 Dec. 1869, https://digital.library.illinois.edu/items/8670fdf0-02dd-013a-7ab5-02d0d7bfd6e4-0. Illinois Library Digital Collections.

Payn, James. Letter from James Payn to Charles E. Mudie, 12 July c. 1877, https://digital.library.illinois.edu/items/867420a0-02dd-013a-7ab5-02d0d7bfd6e4-5.

Preston, William C. 'Mudie's Library'. *Good Words*, edited by Donald MacLeod. Isbister and Company, 1894, pp. 668–98.

Publisher's Circular. 'A Representative Librarian: Mr. W. Faux'. *The Publishers' Circular and Booksellers' Record of British and Foreign Literature*, no. 1293, 11 Apr. 1891.

Punch. 'A Novel Fact'. *Punch Magazine*, 21 Dec. 1867, p. 251.

Rae, W. Fraser. 'Sensation Novelists: Miss Braddon'. *The North British Review*, vol. 43, no. 85, Sept. 1865, 180–204.

Randolph, Mrs. *Genista*. Hurst & Blackett, 1879.

Reade, Charles. *Readiana: Comments on Current Events*. Chatto and Windus, 1883.

Riddell, Allen, and Troy J. Bassett. 'What Library Digitization Leaves Out: Predicting the Availability of Digital Surrogates of English Novels'. *Portal: Libraries and the Academy*, vol. 21, no. 4, 2021, pp. 885–900.

Roberts, Lewis. 'Trafficking in Literary Authority: Mudie's Select Library and the Commodification of the Victorian Novel'. *Victorian Literature and Culture*, vol. 34, no. 1, 2006, pp. 1–25.

Sadler, Glenn Edward. 'MacDonald, George (1824–1905), Poet and Novelist'. *Oxford Dictionary of National Biography*. Oxford University Press, 2004.

Rae, W. Fraser. 'Sensation Novelists: Miss Braddon'. *The North British Review*, vol. 43, no. 85, Sept. 1865.

Riddell, Charlotte. *Did He Deserve It?* Downey & Co., 1897.

Shattock, Joanne. 'The Publishing Industry'. *The Nineteenth-Century Novel, 1820–1880*, edited by John Kucich and Jenny Bourne Taylor. Oxford University Press, 2012, pp. 3–21.

Sutherland, John. 'The Economics of the Victorian Three-Volume Novel', *Business Archives*, vol. 41, 1976, pp. 25–30.

Taylor, John Tinnon. *Early Opposition to the English Novel: The Popular Reaction from 1760 to 1830.* King's Crown Press, 1943.

Tinsley, William. *Random Recollections of an Old Publisher.* Simpkin, Marshall, Hamilton, Kent & Co., 1900.

Times. 'Fire at Mudie's Library: Many Books Destroyed'. *The Times*, 40232nd ed., 7 June 1913, p. 10.

Tuchman, Gaye. *Edging Women Out: Victorian Novelists, Publishers and Social Change.* Routledge, 2012.

Underwood, Ted. *Distant Horizons: Digital Evidence and Literary Change.* University of Chicago Press, 2019.

Wade, Karen, and Porscha Fermanis. 'Reading Across Colonies: Fiction Holdings and Circulating Libraries in the British Southern Hemisphere, 1820–1870'. *Book History*, vol. 26, no. 1, 2023, pp. 71–112.

Wade, Karen, Lauren Cassidy, and Derek Greene. *Mudie's Select Library Catalogues, 1848–1907.* Harvard Dataverse, 30 May 2024. dataverse.harvard.edu, https://doi.org/10.7910/DVN/1YCFXZ.

Ward, Mrs. Humphry. 1918. *A Writer's Recollections.* New York: Harper.

Weedon, Alexis. 'The Uses of Quantification'. *Companion to the History of the Book*, edited by Simon Eliot and Jonathan Rose, John Wiley & Sons, 2019, pp. 33–49.

Williams, Abigail. *The Social Life of Books: Reading Together in the Eighteenth-Century Home.* Yale University Press, 2017.

Wilson, Nicola. 'Boots Book-Lovers' Library and the Novel: The Impact of a Circulating Library Market on Twentieth-Century Fiction'. *Information & Culture*, vol. 49, no. 4, 2014, pp. 427–49.

Wynter, Andrew. 'Mudie's Circulating Library'. *Once a Week*, 21 Dec. 1861.

Mudie's library catalogues in the study

Mudie's Select Library. *A Catalogue of New and Standard Works in Mudie's Select Library, No. 28 Upper King Street, Bloomsbury Square, with Supplementary Catalogue to Mudie's Select Library, March 1849.* Mudie's Select Library, 1848.

Mudie's Select Library. *Catalogue of New and Standard Works in Mudie's Select Library, 509, 510 & 511, New Oxford Street, and 20 & 21 Museum Street, London November 1857.* Mudie's Select Library, 1857.

Mudie, Charles Edward, and Mudie's Select Library. *Catalogue of New and Standard Works in Mudie's Select Library.* Mudie's Select Library, 1860.

Mudie's Select Library. *Catalogue of the Principal Books in Circulation at Mudie's Select Library. Mudie's Select Library*, 1865.

Mudie's Select Library. *Catalogue of the Principal Books in Circulation at Mudie's Select Library. Mudie's Select Library*, 1876.

Mudie's Select Library. *Catalogue of the Principal Books in Circulation at Mudie's Select Library. Mudie's Select Library*, 1885.

Mudie's Select Library. *Catalogue of the Principal Books in Circulation at Mudie's Select Library, January, 1895.* Mudie's Select Library, 1895.

Parsons, Henry G., and Mudie's Select Library. *Catalogue of the Principal English Books in Circulation at Mudie's Select Library.* Mudie's Select Library, 1907.

Acknowledgements

This project has received funding from the European Research Council (ERC) under the European Union's Horizon 2020 research and innovation programme (grant agreement No 884951).

Cambridge Elements ☰

Publishing and Book Culture

SERIES EDITOR
Samantha J. Rayner
University College London

Samantha J. Rayner is Professor of Publishing and Book Cultures
at UCL. She is also Director of UCL's Centre for Publishing,
co-Director of the Bloomsbury CHAPTER (Communication
History, Authorship, Publishing, Textual Editing and
Reading) and co-Chair of the Bookselling Research Network.

ASSOCIATE EDITOR
Leah Tether
University of Bristol

Leah Tether is Professor of Medieval Literature and Publishing
at the University of Bristol. With an academic background in
medieval French and English literature and a professional
background in trade publishing, Leah has combined her
expertise and developed an international research profile in
book and publishing history from manuscript to digital.

ABOUT THE SERIES

This series aims to fill the demand for easily accessible, quality texts available for teaching and research in the diverse and dynamic fields of Publishing and Book Culture. Rigorously researched and peer-reviewed Elements will be published under themes, or 'Gatherings'. These Elements should be the first check point for researchers or students working on that area of publishing and book trade history and practice: we hope that, situated so logically at Cambridge University Press, where academic publishing in the UK began, it will develop to create an unrivalled space where these histories and practices can be investigated and preserved.

Publishing and Book Culture

Publishing and Book History

Gathering Editor: Andrew Nash

Andrew Nash is Reader in Book History and Director of the London Rare Books School at the Institute of English Studies, University of London. He has written books on Scottish and Victorian Literature, and edited or co-edited numerous volumes including, most recently, *The Cambridge History of the Book in Britain, Volume 7* (Cambridge University Press, 2019).

Gathering Editor: Leah Tether

Leah Tether is Professor of Medieval Literature and Publishing at the University of Bristol. With an academic background in medieval French and English literature and a professional background in trade publishing, Leah has combined her expertise and developed an international research profile in book and publishing history from manuscript to digital.

ELEMENTS IN THE GATHERING

Publication and the Papacy in Late Antique and Medieval Europe
Samu Niskanen

Publishing in Wales: Renaissance and Resistance
Jacob D. Rawlins

The People of Print: Seventeenth-Century England
Rachel Stenner, Kaley Kramer and Adam James Smith *et al.*

Publishing in a Medieval Monastery: The View from Twelfth-Century Engelberg
Benjamin Pohl

Communicating the News in Early Modern Europe
Jenni Hyde, Massimo Rospocher, Joad Raymond, Yann Ryan,
Hannu Salmi and Alexandra Schäfer-Griebel

Printing Technologies and Book Production in Seventeenth-Century Japan
Peter Kornicki

Unprinted: Publication Beyond the Press
Daria Kohler and Daniel Wakelin *et al.*

Mudie's Select Library and the Shelf Life of the Nineteenth-Century Novel
Karen Wade

A full series listing is available at: www.cambridge.org/EPBC

Printed in the United States
by Baker & Taylor Publisher Services